THINK THROUGH

WHERE TO **FOCUS**?
WHAT TO **LEARN**?
QUESTIONS TO **ASK**?

EARLY STAGES OF CAREER

ABHISHEK DEOCHAKE

INDIA • SINGAPORE • MALAYSIA

ISBN 979-8-89233-358-0

Purpose of this Book

When reminiscing about the past, people often find themselves pondering what could have been if they possessed certain insights during the early years of their careers. These reflections often revolve around the notion that life could have taken a more positive trajectory. We've all learned through the tough process of trial and error, forging ahead step by step. While there's nothing inherently wrong with this method of advancement, imagine if there were a way to optimize it—a set of guidelines and thought-provoking questions that could act as a pilot through the maze of career exploration. That's precisely what we envisioned, prompting us to delve into research and draw from our own experiences to enhance this trial-and-error approach. Our goal was to offer invaluable nuggets of wisdom to ambitious young individuals embarking on their career journeys—a code to decipher the complex puzzle of professional life right from the start.

It's evident that numerous industries are filled with skilled individuals who lack a clear career trajectory. Not everyone is fortunate enough to encounter a supportive boss or mentor early on, but we firmly believe that even in the absence of such guidance, there's immense potential to thrive during this phase. By focusing on targeted areas of learning and posing pertinent questions to colleagues and superiors, one can navigate this phase with purpose.

Our aim extends beyond simply steering individuals toward on-the-job learning; it's about empowering the idea that even in the absence of a mentor, you can take control and ensure your future self won't look back with regret on decisions made in the corporate world. Every company and industry contributes unique values to your experience, akin to a cross-selling application for life.

We exist in a society where your career choices are subject to judgment, and personal success is measured by its trajectory. Like many, we've experienced the pressure that accompanies early career stages. Instead of excitement and curiosity, it's often anxiety and panic that dominate. The transition from academia to the professional realm can be compared to a toddler's first steps—achieving independence in the world brings euphoria. Our aspiration is for all graduates to reveal a similar sentiment.

While this book primarily caters to a specific demographic (ages 20 to 26), the pursuit of knowledge knows no age bounds—whether one aims to pivot their career based on interests or broaden their general understanding. Many embark on new career journeys later in life or transition from traditional sectors to novel ventures. We've also considered the fact that numerous books tackle the path to entrepreneurship; however, most individuals begin as employees, even if they eventually take the entrepreneurial route.

In the early stages of a career, the art of asking pertinent questions is a skill often underestimated, one that takes years to master. At this juncture, individuals may lack awareness of which questions are meaningful due to a foundational knowledge gap. To address this, we've compiled a question bank at the end of each chapter, kickstarting the process and allowing readers to delve deeper into specific topics as their learning journey progresses. (Our book features over 200 questions tailored to heighten your awareness of your company and industry)

The initial portion of the book focuses on establishing a foundational understanding of essential elements such as companies, job profiles, businesses, and market dynamics. Here, readers delve into crucial knowledge that forms the basis for navigating the professional landscape.

Transitioning to the second half, the narrative shifts towards cultivating awareness regarding one's work, fostering a distinct professional identity, and navigating through career transitions. This segment emphasizes the development of a more nuanced and self-aware approach to the intricacies of the professional journey.

We also aspire to offer graduates a philosophical perspective on careers by presenting an example. Before we plunge into the captivating content of this book, let's ponder: The average human lifespan hovers around 80 years, of which approximately 40 years are devoted to work. Considering a standard routine of 8 hours a day for 5 days a week across 52 weeks (excluding vacations and holidays), the actual work time spent working accumulates to roughly 3000-4000 days, or about 10 years. This perspective unveils the reality that we dedicate a mere 10-15% of our lifespan in the context of time to work—far less than we often stress about.

How to Navigate this Book?

This guide is tailored to cater to individuals at various stages of their early careers. Recognising the diverse beginnings professionals might have, we've structured the content to address the specific needs of each phase. Make revisiting this book a habit, returning to its pages whenever the need arises. Consider it not as a one-time, cover-to-cover read but as a valuable resource to consult.

Launching your Career: If you find yourself in the final year of your university journey, gearing up for placements, embarking on your first internship, or about to step into your initial job, this book is your comprehensive guide. Embrace it as you would a valuable resource, considering yourself a blank canvas with endless opportunities to absorb knowledge across diverse areas without preconceived judgments.

1-4 Years into your Career: For those navigating their first year of employment, undergoing several job changes within a short span, or possessing a keen understanding of specific subjects to explore in terms of skills, aspirations, or knowledge, a personalised approach is encouraged. Feel free to skip certain subcategories or chapters that align with your already mastered skills. Recognise that learning capacities differ, and your timeline for mastering each topic may vary based on your unique understanding and experiences within the industry and company of your choice.

Specialised Domain Focus: Individuals certain about the career path they wish to pursue, such as finance, marketing, engineering, or sales, can streamline their reading experience. Skip chapters and subcategories that don't align with your immediate goals but consider exploring those relevant to potential industry or departmental shifts. Tailor your exploration based on topics that offer maximum career development benefits.

Question Bank for Reflection: Irrespective of your career phase or domain, a set of thought-provoking questions is provided. Whether you're well-versed in the basics or seeking to test your knowledge about your company and industry, these questions serve as valuable tools. Employ them in job interviews to better understand your prospective employer or gauge your reporting manager's influence on your short-term career trajectory. The questions in the final chapter are particularly beneficial for those contemplating a career transition, prompting reflection on the direction and evolution of your professional journey.

Disclaimer: Examples given in the book are only for understanding purposes. Companies, industries, leadership, markets, processes, and methods are always evolving and changing depending on various factors.

Contents

Chapter I

Organization Blueprint: Navigating Structure

Why this Chapter?

In this chapter, we delve into three pivotal subjects—Hierarchy, Culture, and Department—an initial trio that might seem surprising when considered as essential foundations for understanding an organisation's framework at the outset of one's career journey. Drawing from my own professional experiences, I've encountered three distinct phases of career evolution, each marked by shifts in structure. By recounting these shifts, I aim to illuminate why grasping these topics can profoundly impact your self-awareness and career trajectory.

My journey embarked within the Merchant Navy, a realm dominated by significant shipping conglomerates—a realm where hierarchy, culture, and departmental dynamics take on a rigid and unique form. Navigating this world, the learning curve was steep, shaped by stringent regulations aboard ships and an isolated work sphere. The broader scope of departments remained elusive, confined by limited interactions. It took years of immersion to grasp the intricacies of every department and their functions within the shipping company. Notably, the hierarchical and cultural norms diverged starkly from those of shore-based shipping roles. Even considering a transition to a shoreside position within the same company bore witness to a jarring culture shift, redefining work dynamics. This experience underscores that career shifts—whether within the same industry or beyond—demand an understanding of these crucial factors to make informed decisions.

Transitioning into the role of a Naval Architect, specialising in Oil & Gas engineering projects, necessitated drawing upon the context garnered from my prior experiences. Despite this, a host of novel insights awaited, particularly in the spheres of culture and departmental intricacies. The contours of various departments, along with their subcategories tailored to industry requirements, came to the forefront. Engaging in this distinct profile expanded my industry perspective and unveiled hitherto unexplored departments, offering a playground for innovative ideas. While my entrepreneurial endeavour stemming from these insights didn't succeed, it underscored a limitation in my understanding—an understanding confined to specific departments, lacking a comprehensive grasp of the entire corporate landscape.

The present phase of my journey revolves around the dynamic universe of startups. My involvement spans Indian startups and foreign startups of varying sizes. These diverse experiences serve as immersive classrooms for understanding hierarchy, culture, and departmental dynamics across contrasting contexts. The startup realm paints an intricate canvas, revealing the evolution of these foundational elements. Particularly illuminating are experiences within nascent startups, where departments and cultures crystallise based on functional needs and the company's growth stage.

In the symphony of one's career, the chords of Hierarchy, Culture, and Department arrange a melody that echoes across industries and roles. Embracing their significance early on can transform a career trajectory from a simple path into a masterpiece—a journey that resonates with harmonious success.

A: Decoding Hierarchy and Power

Hierarchy refers to the way in which an organisation is structured, with different levels of authority and responsibility. The hierarchy of an organisation can have a significant impact on how work is carried out and how decisions are made.

Large Corporation

A large corporation typically has a complex hierarchy with many different levels of management. At the top of the hierarchy, you have the CEO, followed by the board of directors, executive management, and then various departments, such as marketing, finance, and operations. Each department may have its own hierarchy, with team leaders, managers, and supervisors. This hierarchical structure helps the corporation to operate efficiently and effectively.

Functional Hierarchy: This structure is organised by function or department, with each department headed by a senior manager who reports to a higher-level executive. For example, in a manufacturing company, there may be departments for production, logistics, quality control, marketing, and finance, each with its own manager who reports to the CEO or COO.

Divisional Hierarchy: In this structure, the company is divided into different business units or divisions, each with its own hierarchy. Each division operates independently and has its own goals, strategy, and budget. For example, a consumer goods company may have divisions for food, personal care, and household products, each with its own division head who reports to the CEO.

Matrix Hierarchy: This structure combines elements of both functional and divisional hierarchies. In a matrix structure, employees have two bosses: one who manages them based on their function or expertise, and another who manages them based on their project or division. For example, in a consulting firm, a consultant may be managed by a functional manager in their area of expertise (e.g., strategy) and also by a project manager who oversees the client project they are working on.

Examples

Functional Hierarchy: Procter & Gamble, General Electric, Coca-Cola.

Divisional Hierarchy: General Motors, IBM, Johnson & Johnson.

Matrix Hierarchy: McKinsey & Company, Accenture, Deloitte.

Startups

Flat Hierarchy: Some startups prefer a flat hierarchy where everyone is treated equally and there are no defined levels or titles. In this structure, decision-making is decentralised, and everyone is encouraged to contribute their ideas and opinions.

Zappos: The online shoe retailer is known for its flat hierarchy, where employees are encouraged to be creative and innovative, and decisions are made through consensus rather than by a single person or group.

Functional Hierarchy: In a functional hierarchy, there are different departments based on specific functions, such as marketing, sales, operations, and finance. Each department has a team lead or manager who reports to the CEO or a senior leader.

Dropbox: The cloud storage company has a functional hierarchy, with teams organised by function such as engineering, product, and design. This allows for clear lines of responsibility and efficient decision-making within each department.

Holacracy: Holacracy is a self-management practice where there are no traditional job titles or managers. Instead, roles and responsibilities are defined based on the company's objectives and are constantly changing based on the needs of the business.

Medium: The online publishing platform operates under a unique system called Holacracy, where there are no traditional job titles or managers. Instead, teams are self-organised, and decision-making is decentralised.

Inverted Hierarchy: An inverted hierarchy, also known as a flat hierarchy, flips the traditional organisational structure by decentralising decision-making and reducing the number of management layers. This approach promotes open communication, collaborative culture, and employee empowerment, fostering a more agile and responsive organisation. It contrasts with the traditional pyramid-shaped hierarchy, emphasising flexibility and adaptability in a rapidly changing business environment.

Buffer: The social media management platform has an inverted hierarchy, where the CEO is at the bottom of the pyramid and employees at the top. This approach is designed to empower employees to take ownership of their work and decision-making.

Hybrid Hierarchy: A hybrid hierarchy combines elements of both traditional and modern organisational structures, aiming to leverage the strengths of each approach. It typically features a mix of hierarchical levels for managerial control and clear reporting lines while also incorporating elements of flexibility and collaboration seen in flat or agile structures. This structure is designed to provide stability and order, typical of traditional hierarchies, while also allowing for adaptability and innovation in response to dynamic business environments. Companies adopting a hybrid hierarchy seek to strike a balance between the efficiency of a traditional hierarchy and the agility of more contemporary organisational models.

Asana: The project management software company has a hybrid hierarchy, combining elements of both functional and flat hierarchies. Teams are organised by function, but decision-making is shared across the company, and there is a strong emphasis on transparency and open communication.

Small Business

In a small business, the hierarchy is often much simpler, with fewer levels of management. The owner or CEO may be the only person at the top of the hierarchy, followed by a few managers or supervisors. Because there are fewer people involved in the decision-making process, small businesses can often be more nimble and adaptable.

Traditional Sector

Military: The military is a prime example of a hierarchical organisation where the chain of command is crucial for maintaining order and discipline. The military hierarchy is based on rank, with commissioned officers at the top, followed by non-commissioned officers and enlisted personnel at the bottom. Within each rank, seniority plays a role in determining the hierarchy. For example, a senior captain may have more authority than a junior captain.

Law: Law firms typically have partners at the top and associates at the bottom. Partners are the owners of the firm and have the highest authority, with associates working under their supervision. Within the partnership, there may be further hierarchies based on seniority or area of expertise, such as senior partners or managing partners.

Education: Educational institutions have a clear hierarchy, with principals, vice principals, and department heads at the top, followed by teachers and support staff. The principal is responsible for the overall management and direction of the school, with vice principals and department heads supporting them in their roles. Teachers are responsible for delivering the curriculum, while support staff provides administrative and logistical support.

Government: Government organisations have elected officials at the top and civil servants at the bottom. Elected officials, such as the president, governor, or mayor, have the highest authority and are responsible for setting policy and direction. Civil servants, such as bureaucrats and administrators, implement these policies and provide support to elected officials. Within each level, there may be further hierarchies based on seniority or area of responsibility, such as cabinet members or agency heads.

Healthcare: Healthcare organisations have doctors at the top, followed by nurses, allied health professionals, and administrative staff. Doctors are responsible for diagnosing and treating patients, with nurses providing support and assistance. Allied health professionals, such as physical therapists and occupational therapists, work in specialised areas to provide additional support. Administrative staff provides logistical and organisational support, such as scheduling appointments and managing medical records. Within each profession, there may be further hierarchies based on specialisation, seniority, or clinical experience, such as chief of staff or head of nursing.

B: Unveiling Cultural Foundations

In the context of work, culture refers to the shared values, beliefs, attitudes, and behaviours that exist within an organisation. It encompasses the character and personality of the organisation, shaping its unique identity. Here are some key points about work culture:

Behaviour and Attitudes: Work culture is reflected in the ways people in the organisation behave and interact with each other. It includes both formal, stated norms and implicit ways of working. It influences how employees approach their work and how they interact with colleagues.

Values and Beliefs: Culture is shaped by the values and beliefs that are shared among employees. These values guide decision-making, actions, and priorities within the organisation.

Organisational Climate: Work culture creates the overall atmosphere and environment in the workplace. It affects the level of engagement, satisfaction, and productivity of employees.

Alignment with Goals: A strong and positive work culture is important because it supports and advances the company's goals and strategies. It helps attract and retain talented individuals who align with the organisation's values.

Employee Influence: Employees play a role in shaping and maintaining the work culture. They can provide input and feedback on the desired culture, participate in culture-building programs, and adhere to the routines and norms that interpret the desired culture.

Types of Culture

Hierarchical Culture: In this culture, there is a clear hierarchy of power and authority. Decisions are made at the top, and employees at lower levels are expected to follow orders. This culture can be found in many traditional organisations, such as banks and law firms.

Example: Goldman Sachs, a multinational investment bank, has a hierarchical culture where decision-making power is concentrated at the top, with senior executives holding a significant amount of control over the company's operations.

Clan Culture: This culture is focused on the employees and their relationships with each other. The company is like a family, and employees are encouraged to work collaboratively and share common goals. This culture is often found in companies that prioritise teamwork and employee engagement.

Example: Google, a multinational technology company, has a clan culture where employees are encouraged to collaborate and share ideas freely. The company offers many perks and benefits to keep employees engaged and motivated.

Market Culture: In this culture, the emphasis lies in accomplishing objectives and outcomes. Competition is encouraged, and employees are rewarded for their individual contributions to the company's success. This culture is often found in sales-driven organisations.

Example: Amazon, a multinational e-commerce company, has a market culture where employees are driven to achieve results and compete with each other to meet their targets. The company has a strong focus on data-driven decision-making and measures the performance of its employees through metrics.

Adhocracy Culture: This culture places its emphasis on innovation and adaptability. Employees are encouraged to take risks and come up with new ideas to drive the company forward. This culture is often found in startups and companies in fast-paced industries.

Example: Apple, a multinational technology company, has an adhocracy culture where employees are encouraged to think creatively and take risks. The company has a reputation for innovation and is known for disrupting industries with new products and technologies.

Bureaucratic Culture: In this culture, the central focus is on compliance with regulations and established protocols. The company is highly structured and formal, and employees are expected to follow established processes and protocols. This culture is often found in government organisations and other heavily regulated industries.

Example: IBM, a multinational technology company, has a bureaucratic culture where employees are expected to follow established procedures and protocols. The company is known for its rigorous approach to project management and product development.

Innovative Culture: Startups that are focused on developing new technologies or products often have an innovative culture. These companies tend to be highly adaptable and willing to take risks to bring their ideas to market. Employees in these startups are often encouraged to think creatively and share their ideas freely, with a focus on finding new solutions to problems.

Example: Tesla is a well-known startup with an innovative culture. The company is focused on developing new technologies for electric vehicles, renewable energy, and energy storage, and encourages its employees to think outside the box to solve problems and push the boundaries of what is possible.

Collaborative Culture: Startups that place a high value on collaboration tend to have a culture that emphasises teamwork and open communication. These companies often have a flat organisational structure, where employees at all levels are encouraged to contribute ideas and work together to achieve the company's goals.

Example: Asana is a startup that has a collaborative culture. The company provides project management software that helps teams work together more efficiently and effectively and encourages its employees to work in cross-functional teams to develop new features and improve the product.

Customer-Oriented Culture: Startups that are focused on delivering the best possible experience for their customers often have a customer-oriented culture. These companies prioritise customer feedback and use it to drive product development, marketing, and other business decisions.

Example: Airbnb is a startup that has a strong customer-oriented culture. The company is focused on providing unique and memorable travel experiences for its customers and uses customer feedback to improve its platform and develop new features that better meet the needs of its users.

Agile Culture: Startups that value agility tend to have a culture that emphasises flexibility and responsiveness. These companies are able to quickly adapt to changes in the market or shifts in customer needs and are willing to pivot their business model or strategy as needed.

Example: Slack is a startup that has an agile culture. The company provides a messaging platform for teams and is focused on making it easier for employees to communicate and collaborate. Slack is known for its ability to quickly iterate and improve its product based on customer feedback and market trends.

Fun Culture: Startups that place a high value on employee happiness and work-life balance often have a fun culture. These companies create a relaxed and enjoyable work environment and prioritise activities like team building, social events, and perks like free snacks or company outings.

Example: Zappos is a startup that has a fun culture. The company is focused on providing exceptional customer service but also places a high value on employee happiness and well-being. Zappos is known for its quirky and relaxed work environment and offers a variety of employee perks like free lunches, company outings, and on-site amenities like a fitness centre and massage therapist.

Traditional Sector

Law: Law firms are known for having a competitive and intense culture, often with a focus on billable hours and meeting targets. There may also be a strong emphasis on professionalism and maintaining a certain image. Examples of law firms known for their culture include Skadden, Arps, Slate, Meagher & Flom, and Cravath, Swaine & Moore.

Education: Educational institutions often have a culture of collaboration and teamwork, with an emphasis on learning and personal growth. However, there may also be a bureaucratic or hierarchical culture, particularly in larger institutions. Examples of educational institutions with distinctive cultures include Harvard University and Stanford University.

Government: Government organizations can have a culture of bureaucracy and red tape, with a focus on following procedures and regulations. However, there may also be a sense of public service and a commitment to serving the community. Examples of government organizations with distinctive cultures include the United States Department of State and the United Kingdom's Foreign and Commonwealth Office.

Defense: The defence industry often has a culture of discipline and order, with a focus on following strict procedures and protocols. There may also be a sense of patriotism and duty, particularly among military personnel. Examples of defence companies with distinctive cultures include Lockheed Martin and Raytheon.

Small Businesses: Traditional businesses can have a range of cultures depending on the industry and company. However, there may be a focus on stability, long-term planning, and a commitment to the company's values and mission. Examples of small businesses with distinctive cultures include family-owned businesses with minimum exposure to funding or decision-making power.

C: Exploring Departments and Their Functions

Human Resources (HR) Department: This department is responsible for managing the organization's employees. The functions of this department include recruiting, hiring, onboarding, training, and development of employees. HR also ensures compliance with labour laws and regulations, maintains employee records, and handles employee relations issues.

Finance and Accounting Department: This department is responsible for managing the company's financial resources. The functions of this department include budgeting, financial planning and analysis, accounting, payroll, tax planning and compliance, and risk management.

Marketing Department: This department is responsible for promoting the company's products or services to potential customers. The functions of this department include market research, branding, advertising, public relations, and sales.

Operations Department: This department is responsible for managing the day-to-day operations of the organization. The functions of this department include production, quality control, supply chain management, inventory management, and logistics.

Information Technology (IT) Department: This department is responsible for managing the company's technology infrastructure. The functions of this department include managing computer hardware and software, network security, data management, and providing technical support to employees.

Research and Development (R&D) Department: This department is responsible for developing new products or improving existing ones. The functions of this department include conducting market research, product design, prototyping, testing, and patenting.

Customer Service Department: This department is responsible for providing customer support and resolving customer issues. The functions of this department include answering customer inquiries, handling complaints, and providing technical support.

Legal Department: This department is responsible for managing the legal affairs of the company. The functions of this department include contract management, regulatory compliance, and handling lawsuits.

Administrative Department: This department is responsible for managing the day-to-day administrative tasks of the company. The functions of this department include managing office supplies, equipment, and facilities, scheduling appointments, and coordinating meetings.

Sales Department: This department is responsible for generating revenue for the company through sales of its products or services. The functions of this department include lead generation, sales prospecting, sales closing, and account management.

Conclusion

"Decoding Hierarchy and Power" unveils the dynamic nature of organizational authority. Recognising hierarchy as more than titles, it emphasises a nuanced view of both formal and informal power structures. Understanding diverse forms of power enables strategic positioning within the organisation, fostering collaboration and informed decision-making. Usually, all the companies operate with multiple hierarchies and cultures that are suitable. They are not restricted to just one, as it also helps them navigate and learn as per the stage at which it is being operated.

"Unveiling Cultural Foundations" highlights organisational culture as a driving force. Understanding and aligning with cultural values fosters a cohesive, purpose-driven environment. Leaders are urged to shape culture towards inclusivity, adaptability, and resilience.

"Exploring Departments and Their Function" emphasises the importance of cross-functional collaboration. Breaking down silos and understanding each department's unique role fosters a holistic view, promoting a culture where information flows freely and collective goals supersede departmental interests. These are very generic departments; some companies, depending on the industries and specific domains, could have more departments as per requirements. We will discuss these in more detail in Chapter IV with respect to the actual role of the employee, so you can get more clarity on the specific role you may wish to learn and upgrade your skill set for such responsibilities.

D: Effective Questions to Ask the Leaders

- How does the company's hierarchy work, and what is the chain of command?
- What is the process for promotions and moving up in the hierarchy?
- How does seniority play a role in determining hierarchy in the company?
- Can you explain the difference between a manager and a supervisor in the company?
- How does the company ensure accountability among employees at different levels of the hierarchy?
- How would you describe the company culture, and what values are important to the company?
- How does the company encourage teamwork and collaboration among employees?
- What is the company's approach to work-life balance, and how is this supported?
- How does the company handle conflicts or differences in opinions among employees?
- What opportunities does the company offer for professional development and growth?
- Can you explain the different departments within the company and their functions?
- How do the different departments within the company work together to achieve company goals?
- How does the company measure the success of each department?

- What is the process for employees to move between departments within the company?
- Can you explain the role of support departments, such as HR and IT, in the company?
- How does the company ensure that all employees are treated fairly, regardless of their position in the hierarchy?
- What steps does the company take to promote diversity and inclusion in the workplace?
- How does the company handle employee feedback and suggestions for improvement?
- How does the company recognize and reward employees for their achievements and contributions?
- Can you share any examples of how the company has successfully adapted to changes in the industry or market in the context of culture?

Chapter II

Uncovering Power Dynamics

Why this Chapter?

Within the realm of work, power dynamics remain an enigmatic force, often overlooked but wielding significant influence. This chapter serves as your compass, guiding you through the web of organizational dynamics. It unveils the art of identifying key individuals to seek out based on the intricacies of your circumstances and, equally crucially, those you'd do well to steer clear of. Not every challenge or situation demands escalation to your immediate supervisor. In fact, the intricacies of certain scenarios necessitate the involvement of individuals who possess the precise alignment of power and intent.

Delving into the heart of leadership styles, decision-making authorities, power dynamics' architects, and pivotal internal stakeholders, this chapter illuminates a roadmap for optimal navigation. Mastering the art of reaching out to the right individuals can drastically alter the trajectory of your career, influencing not only the current situation but also your growth trajectory.

Reflecting on my own journey, I've encountered instances where a different course could have been charted had I sought counsel from individuals wielding the appropriate power. These figures possess the potential to breathe life into your ideas, untangle your predicaments, impart valuable skills, and provide guidance for future strides—be it pursuing higher education, embracing a new professional realm, or pivoting within the organization.

Awareness of these dynamics acts as a beacon, illuminating the path to those who hold the reins that matter. It's not uncommon for your immediate manager to be oblivious to certain organizational facets. Even if well-intentioned, they might lack the visibility to advance your objectives or champion your ideas effectively. This underscores the importance of identifying and approaching individuals whose position and influence align with your goals.

In the intricate shade of organizational dynamics, recognizing power and intent can be your greatest ally. By deciphering this harmony, you'll orchestrate your journey with precision, aligning with those who can wield the right notes to elevate your career.

A: Leadership Awareness

Explanation of different leadership styles in large corporations and startups

Autocratic Leadership: This style of leadership involves making decisions independently without involving employees in the decision-making process. Leaders who follow this style tend to be authoritative, with little room for employee input. Examples of companies with autocratic leadership include Apple Inc. and Amazon.

Transformational Leadership: Transformational leaders inspire and motivate their employees to achieve common goals, often by setting a vision for the organization and inspiring employees to work towards that vision. They also focus on employee development and encourage creativity and innovation. Examples of companies with transformational leadership include Google and Microsoft.

Servant Leadership: In this style, the leader's primary focus is on serving their employees and meeting their needs. Servant leaders believe that by taking care of their employees, they will, in turn, take care of the company and its customers. Examples of companies with servant leadership include the Ritz-Carlton Hotel Company and Southwest Airlines.

Democratic Leadership: Democratic leaders involve their employees in the decision-making process and value their input. They encourage open communication and collaboration among team members. Examples of companies with democratic leadership include Ford Motor Company and General Electric.

Laissez-faire Leadership: Laissez-faire leaders give employees the freedom to make decisions and work independently. They provide minimal guidance and are typically hands-off in their approach to leadership. Examples of companies with laissez-faire leadership include Google and Zappos.

Transactional Leadership: Transactional leaders set clear expectations and reward employees for meeting those expectations. They focus on achieving specific goals and use a system of rewards and punishments to motivate employees. Examples of companies with transactional leadership include Walmart and Coca-Cola.

Situational Leadership: Situational leaders adapt their leadership style based on the situation at hand and the needs of their employees. They may switch between different leadership styles as needed. Examples of companies with situational leadership include IBM and Procter & Gamble.

Charismatic Leadership: Charismatic leaders have a magnetic personality and can inspire and motivate their employees through their words and actions. They often have a strong vision for the future and are skilled at communicating that vision to their team. Examples of companies with charismatic leadership include Tesla and Virgin Group.

Bureaucratic Leadership: Bureaucratic leaders rely heavily on rules, policies, and procedures to make decisions. They value stability and consistency over creativity and innovation. Examples of companies with bureaucratic leadership include Ford and McDonald's.

Authentic Leadership: Authentic leaders are true to themselves and their values, and they lead by example. They prioritize transparency, honesty, and ethical behavior. Examples of companies with authentic leadership include Patagonia and Ben & Jerry's.

Traditional Sector

Education: In the education sector, a democratic leadership style may be effective, where leaders involve teachers and staff in decision-making processes. This helps to create a sense of ownership and fosters a collaborative environment. For example, a principal may hold regular meetings with teachers to discuss policies and procedures and actively seek feedback on how to improve the school.

Defense: In the defence sector, a directive leadership style is often used. This involves leaders giving clear instructions and expecting immediate compliance. This style is necessary in high-risk situations where there is little room for error. For example, a commanding officer may give orders to troops during a military operation with the expectation that they will be followed without question.

Law: In the legal sector, a transformational leadership style may be effective, where leaders inspire and motivate their team to work towards a common goal. This style emphasizes the importance of developing and nurturing relationships with clients and colleagues. For example, a senior partner in a law firm may mentor and coach junior associates, providing guidance and support as they develop their legal skills.

Healthcare: In the healthcare sector, a servant leadership style may be effective, where leaders focus on serving their patients and the community. This style emphasizes empathy, active listening, and a deep commitment to patient care. For example, a hospital administrator may work to create a culture of patient-centred care where staff are encouraged to go above and beyond to meet the needs of their patients.

Government: In the government sector, a bureaucratic leadership style may be effective, where leaders follow established rules and procedures to ensure consistency and predictability in decision-making. This style emphasizes adherence to protocols and guidelines and can help to promote transparency and accountability. For example, a department head may ensure that all employees are following established protocols when processing paperwork or making decisions related to public policy.

B: Decision Makers in Action

Large Corporations

Senior Leadership: These decision-makers are responsible for the overall strategy and direction of the company.

Examples of decisions they might make include:

- Whether to expand into new markets or product lines
- Setting the company's long-term goals and objectives
- Making decisions about mergers and acquisitions
- Approving major investments in new technology or infrastructure

Middle Management: These decision-makers are responsible for implementing the company's strategy and overseeing day-to-day operations.

Examples of decisions they might make include:

- Deciding on hiring and firing of employees
- Allocating resources to different projects or departments
- Setting sales goals and targets for individual teams
- Developing and implementing new policies or procedures

Frontline Employees: These decision-makers are responsible for executing the day-to-day tasks of the company.

Examples of decisions they might make include:

- Deciding how to best serve customers in specific situations
- Making decisions about the most efficient way to complete a task
- Prioritizing their work to ensure deadlines are met
- Identifying and reporting problems with products or services to management

Startups

Founders/CEOs: Founders or CEOs are typically the primary decision-makers in startups. They are responsible for setting the company's vision and direction, making key strategic decisions, and allocating resources.

Board of Directors: In some startups, a board of directors may be established to provide oversight and guidance to the CEO. The board may have the power to make important decisions, such as hiring or firing the CEO, approving major investments or acquisitions, and setting executive compensation.

Investors: Investors in startups may have a say in certain decisions, particularly if they hold a significant stake in the company. They may be involved in key decisions such as funding rounds, mergers or acquisitions, and major strategic shifts.

Department Heads: As startups grow and add more employees, decision-making power may become more distributed. Department heads may be responsible for making decisions within their area of expertise, such as product development or marketing.

Team Members: In some startups, decision-making power may be distributed even further, with team members given autonomy to make decisions related to their specific projects or tasks.

Examples of Decisions Made by these Decision-Makers in Startups Include:

Founders/CEOs: Setting the overall vision and strategy for the company, making decisions related to funding and investment, hiring and firing senior executives, and deciding when to pivot or change direction.

Board of Directors: Approving major investments or acquisitions, providing guidance and oversight to the CEO, setting executive compensation, and making decisions related to the company's governance and compliance.

Investors: Deciding whether or not to invest in the company, participating in funding rounds, providing guidance and feedback to the company's leadership team, and advocating for changes in the company's strategy or direction.

Department Heads: Making decisions related to product development, marketing, sales, operations, or other areas of the business within their area of expertise.

Team Members: Making decisions related to specific projects or tasks, such as deciding on design elements, programming languages, or marketing strategies.

Traditional Sector

Education: In K-12 schools, the principal and school board members make decisions on policies, curriculum, and the hiring of teachers and staff. In higher education, decisions are made by the board of trustees, college or university president, and academic deans. They make decisions on budget, admission policies, curriculum, faculty hiring and promotion, and campus infrastructure.

Law: Law firms have a hierarchical structure, and the partners and managing partners make major decisions on business strategy, client acquisition, and hiring. In the court system, judges make decisions on cases based on legal precedent and their interpretation of the law.

Healthcare: In hospitals, major decisions are made by the board of directors, CEO, and department heads. They make decisions on budget, staffing, and patient care policies. In pharmaceutical companies, the executive team and board of directors make decisions on drug development, research and development, and marketing.

Government: In government, elected officials such as the president, governor, and mayor make decisions on policies, budgets, and laws. Civil servants also play a role in decision-making, as they provide expertise and implement policies set by elected officials.

Defense: The military has a strict chain of command, with decisions made by the highest-ranking officers. They make decisions on strategy, deployment, and mission planning. In defense contracting, executives and board members make decisions on contracts, research and development, and partnerships with other companies.

C: Dealing with Power Hoarders

In the context of employee titles in large companies and startups, power hoarders refer to individuals who hold positions of authority and influence within the organisation and tend to withhold power, information, or opportunities for personal gain or control. These individuals prioritise their own interests over the collective success of the organisation and may engage in behaviours that hinder collaboration, stifle innovation, and limit the growth of others.

In large companies, power hoarders can be found at various hierarchical levels, such as senior executives, department heads, or team leaders. They may use their positions to maintain control over resources, decision-making processes, and access to opportunities, often at the expense of other employees. They may resist sharing information, delegate tasks unfairly, or micromanage their subordinates, creating a culture of fear and dependency.

In startups, power hoarders can manifest in different ways due to the less formalised structure and dynamic nature of these organisations. Founders or CEOs who exhibit power hoarding behaviours may make all the important decisions without seeking input or delegating responsibility. They may resist sharing equity or recognition with employees, leading to a lack of empowerment and motivation among the team. In some cases, power hoarders in startups may also try to control all aspects of the business, stifling creativity and limiting the growth potential of the organisation.

Power hoarders, regardless of the organisational context, can have negative impacts on employee morale, productivity, and overall company culture. Their actions can hinder collaboration, discourage initiative, and create a toxic work environment. Recognising and addressing power hoarding behaviours is essential for fostering a healthy and inclusive workplace where power and opportunities are distributed equitably and employees can thrive and contribute their best.

Navigating the challenging terrain of dealing with a power hoarder can indeed be a demanding task. However, armed with some effective strategies, you can begin to address the issue constructively.

Here are some tips to help you in this endeavour:

Communicate: Initiate a dialogue with the power hoarder. Seek to gain insight into their perspective and motivations. Explain how their behaviour is affecting you and your colleagues. The goal here is to foster understanding and, ideally, reach a compromise that benefits everyone involved.

Document: Keep a meticulous record of the power hoarder's actions and behaviours. Note down specific incidents, their consequences on the team or project, and any pertinent details. This documentation can be invaluable should you need to escalate the issue to higher authorities or HR, providing clear evidence of the problem.

Involve others: If the power hoarder's actions are negatively impacting the entire team, consider involving your colleagues in the conversation. Collective action can demonstrate to the power hoarder that their behaviour is not acceptable and can create a united front for addressing the issue.

Seek support: Don't hesitate to reach out for support from a mentor, coach, or therapist if you find yourself struggling to cope with the situation. They can provide guidance on how to manage the challenges you're facing, both professionally and emotionally. Self-care and maintaining your well-being are crucial during this process.

Be patient and persistent: Dealing with a power hoarder can be a lengthy and arduous process. Be prepared for setbacks and resistance along the way. Stay resolute in your efforts to address the issue, and remember that persistence can be a powerful force for change.

Advocate for yourself and your team: Ultimately, it's essential to stand up for yourself and your colleagues. A positive and productive work environment is worth fighting for. By advocating for fairness, transparency, and collaboration, you can contribute to creating a healthier workplace for everyone.

Dealing with a power hoarder is not an easy journey, but it's a necessary one for the sake of your team's well-being and the organisation's success. With patience, persistence, and the right strategies, you can work towards a more harmonious and productive work environment.

D: Harnessing Internal Stakeholder Influence

In the context of large companies and startups, internal stakeholders refer to individuals or groups within the organisation who have a direct interest or involvement in its operations, success, and outcomes. These stakeholders have a vested interest in the organisation's performance and may influence or be influenced by its decisions, strategies, and actions.

In Large Companies:

1. **Employees:** Employees are important internal stakeholders in large companies. They contribute their skills, knowledge, and efforts to the organisation's goals and success. Their satisfaction, engagement, and well-being can significantly impact overall performance.

2. **Managers and Executives:** Managers and executives are responsible for overseeing different departments and functions within the organisation. They play a crucial role in decision-making, setting strategic directions, and ensuring effective execution of plans.

3. **Shareholders/Owners:** Shareholders or owners of the company hold equity in the organisation and have a financial stake in its performance. They may influence decision-making through voting rights and expect returns on their investments.

4. **Board of Directors:** The board of directors provides governance and oversight in large companies. They are responsible for making important decisions, setting policies, and ensuring the company's long-term success.

5. **Trade Unions or Labour Groups:** In organisations with unionised workforces, labour groups represent the interests of employees, negotiate collective bargaining agreements, and advocate for fair treatment and working conditions.

In Startups:

1. **Founders/Entrepreneurs:** Founders or entrepreneurs are key internal stakeholders in startups. They often have a significant personal investment in the company and play a pivotal role in shaping its vision, strategy, and culture.

2. **Early Employees:** Early employees who join startups at an early stage become internal stakeholders. They contribute to the growth and development of the company and often have a close working relationship with the founders.

3. **Investors:** Investors in startups provide financial backing and support. They become internal stakeholders with a vested interest in the company's success and may provide guidance, connections, and resources.

4. **Advisory Board:** Startups may have an advisory board comprising industry experts, mentors, or experienced professionals who provide guidance and expertise in specific areas to support the company's growth and decision-making.

5. **Incubators/Accelerators:** Startups that are part of incubator or accelerator programs have access to mentors, resources, and networks. These organisations become internal stakeholders and provide support for the startup's development.

Internal stakeholders are critical for the success of both large companies and startups. Their involvement, support, and collaboration are crucial for achieving organisational goals, driving innovation, and creating a positive work environment.

Conclusion

"Leadership Awareness" illuminates the pivotal role of self-awareness in effective leadership. Recognising one's influence, strengths, and potential blind spots enhances leadership effectiveness. This section advocates about types of leaders and how they cultivate a keen understanding of their impact on power dynamics, fostering a more transparent and collaborative organisational culture.

"Decision Makers in Action" provides insights into the decision-making process and its impact on power dynamics. Understanding how decisions are made and the individuals driving them allows for strategic engagement. This section encourages individuals to navigate decision-making channels effectively, ensuring their perspectives contribute meaningfully to the organisational discourse. Overall, the decision-making process varies across different sectors and organisations. It can be influenced by factors such as organisational structure, hierarchy, expertise, and external factors like legal and regulatory requirements.

"Dealing with Power Hoarders" addresses the challenge of individuals who consolidate power for personal gain. This section equips readers with strategies to navigate such dynamics, emphasising the importance of open communication, collaboration, and fostering a culture that values shared influence over hoarded power.

"Harnessing Internal Stakeholder Influence" explores the art of leveraging internal relationships for positive organisational impact. Recognising the diverse sources of influence within the organisation and strategically engaging with stakeholders enhances one's ability to drive change. This section underscores the value of building alliances and collaborative networks to amplify collective influence and achieve shared goals.

E: Effective Questions to Ask the Leaders

- Can you explain the organizational structure and hierarchy, and how power is distributed among different levels?
- How would you describe the leadership style in this organisation? How does it impact power dynamics and decision-making?
- Who are the key decision-makers in our team/department/organisation? How do they influence the direction and decision-making processes?

- Are there any power hoarders or individuals who tend to monopolise decision-making or control resources? How does it impact the overall dynamics?
- How are power and authority delegated within our team/department/organisation? Is there a system in place to ensure fairness and transparency?
- Can you share an example of a situation where power dynamics played a significant role in a decision or outcome within our organisation?
- How does the organisation involve internal stakeholders in decision-making processes? Are there mechanisms to gather input and feedback from employees?
- What steps does the organisation take to address power imbalances and promote a more inclusive and collaborative work environment?
- How does the organisation manage conflicts and power struggles among team members or departments?
- Are there any ongoing initiatives or programs aimed at developing leadership skills and fostering a more balanced distribution of power within the organisation?
- Can you provide examples of how leadership styles have evolved over time in this organisation and how it has affected power dynamics?
- How does the organisation handle power transitions, such as leadership changes or promotions? Is there a structured approach in place?
- Are there any specific strategies or practices in place to prevent power hoarding or abuse of power within our organisation?
- How does the organisation encourage and support employees to take on leadership roles and contribute to decision-making processes?
- Are there any mentorship or coaching programs available for employees to develop their leadership skills and navigate power dynamics effectively?
- How are internal stakeholders identified and engaged in strategic decision-making processes?
- Can you share an example of a time when internal stakeholders played a significant role in shaping a decision or strategy?

- What efforts does the organisation make to ensure that power dynamics do not hinder collaboration and teamwork across departments?
- How does the organisation promote a culture of accountability and transparency in decision-making processes?
- Are there any specific measures in place to recognise and reward individuals who actively contribute to a positive and balanced power dynamic within the organisation?

Chapter III

Unravelling Market Forces Dynamics

Why this Chapter?

Grasping the intricacies of market dynamics isn't just a strategic move; it's a cornerstone for those aspiring to take the helm as managers or embarking on diverse career and business endeavours. The term "market dynamics" encompasses the powerful currents that sway a market's course—be it the flow of product or service demand, the nuanced dance between supply and consumer preferences, the ever-shifting competitive panorama, the pulse of economic conditions, or the seismic shifts forced by technological strides.

When I cast my memory back to the early chapters of my career, it's evident that comprehending market dynamics wasn't a notion that immediately commanded my focus. However, hindsight tells me that a far more rewarding learning curve could have unfurled had I anchored my career voyage with an acute understanding of this very topic. The possibilities unfold like a panorama—the prospect to pivot professions with finesse, or even to embark on entrepreneurial pursuits—these could have been catalysed much earlier than initially envisioned. The realisation resonates: by acquainting yourself with market dynamics, one gains the lens to perceive market trends as early sketches of opportunities, which can eventually evolve into full-fledged career shifts or the birth of innovative businesses.

Furthermore, the art of anticipating market fluctuation is akin to deciphering a complex code. It's the aptitude to capture the correlation of consumer desires before they change, and to decode the intricate interplay between economic fluctuations and market responses. Armed with this judgement, decisions become calculated and actions, strategic—a compass guiding your course through the ever-evolving business terrain.

In the grand curtains of a career, the thread of market dynamics is woven intricately. To grip this thread is to wield a key that opens doors to earlier unexplored views—a transformative force that accelerates your trajectory towards realising aspirations once deemed distant.

Switching Departments or Jobs: When transitioning to a new department or job role, understanding the market dynamics of that specific industry or field is essential. This knowledge helps you identify trends, demands, and potential challenges. It allows you to align your skills, experiences, and goals with the market needs, making you a more effective and strategic manager. Additionally, understanding market dynamics enables you to make informed decisions about the types of projects to pursue, the skills to develop, and the strategies to implement for success.

Switching Industries: Moving to a different industry involves adapting to a new set of market dynamics. Each industry has its unique characteristics, customer behaviours, and competitive landscape. By comprehending the market dynamics, you can identify opportunities, potential obstacles, and areas where your skills can create value. This knowledge helps you make informed decisions about resource allocation, marketing strategies, and business development efforts.

Going for Higher Education: Pursuing higher education, such as a master's degree or an MBA, is an investment in your future career. Understanding the market dynamics of the industry you plan to enter after completing your education helps you select the right programme and specialisation. It allows you to acquire relevant skills and knowledge that align with the evolving needs of the market. This preparation can enhance your employability and increase your chances of landing a managerial role in a competitive job market.

Starting a Business: Launching a business requires a deep understanding of market dynamics. You need to identify your target audience, assess demand for your product or service, analyse the competitive landscape, and predict market trends. This information is vital for creating a viable business plan, pricing strategy, and marketing approach. By staying attuned to market dynamics, you can make agile decisions that enable your business to adapt and thrive in a changing environment.

Switching Industry to Start a Business: If you're leaving your current industry to start a business, understanding the market dynamics of your new venture is crucial. You'll need to research your chosen market segment, identify unmet needs, and design products or services that resonate with customers. Knowledge of market trends, consumer behaviour, and potential competitors will inform your business strategy and increase your chances of success.

A: Balancing Supply and Demand

Market dynamics revolve around the relationship between supply and demand. Supply refers to the amount of a product or service that businesses are willing to provide, while demand represents how much consumers are willing to buy. When demand is high and supply is low, prices tend to rise. Conversely, when supply exceeds demand, prices usually decrease.

Example 1: During a holiday season, the demand for toys increases significantly. Toy manufacturers and retailers anticipate this higher demand and increase their supply by producing and stocking up on popular toys. As a result, prices may rise due to the limited supply and increased demand.

Example 2: In the oil industry, when global demand for oil exceeds the available supply, prices tend to rise. This can occur due to factors such as geopolitical tensions, disruptions in oil production, or increased consumption from emerging economies. Conversely, when supply exceeds demand, prices may decrease as producers adjust their output to balance the market.

B: The Dance of Price Fluctuations

Market dynamics are closely tied to price fluctuations. As supply and demand change, prices can go up or down. For example, if there is a shortage of a popular product, its price may increase because people are willing to pay more to get it. On the other hand, if there is an oversupply of a product, prices may drop to encourage more people to buy.

Example 1: In the real estate market, when there is a high demand for housing and limited supply, prices of properties in desirable locations tend to increase. Conversely, during an economic downturn when demand decreases and supply exceeds demand, property prices may decline.

Example 2: The price of agricultural commodities, such as wheat or corn, can fluctuate based on factors like weather conditions, global trade policies, or changes in demand from the food industry. For instance, a drought affecting wheat production can lead to reduced supply, causing prices to rise.

C: Deciphering Consumer Behaviour

Market dynamics are influenced by how consumers behave. Factors such as preferences, tastes, income levels, and trends impact what people buy and how much they are willing to pay. Businesses need to understand consumer behaviour to effectively market their products or services and stay ahead of their competitors.

Example 1: With the increasing concern for environmental sustainability, consumers are becoming more inclined to purchase eco-friendly products. This shift in consumer behaviour has led businesses to develop and market sustainable alternatives, such as biodegradable packaging or electric vehicles.

Example 2: In the smartphone industry, consumer preferences for features like camera quality, processing power, or screen size influence their purchasing decisions. Smartphone manufacturers must stay updated on consumer trends to develop products that meet their demands and stay competitive.

D: Triumphing Amidst Competition

Competition plays a vital role in market dynamics. When there are multiple businesses offering similar products or services, they compete for customers. This competition drives innovation, better quality, and lower prices. Businesses need to understand their competitors, their strengths, and weaknesses to differentiate themselves and attract customers.

Example 1: In the fast-food industry, major chains like McDonald's, Burger King, and Wendy's compete for customers by offering competitive pricing, new menu items, or innovative marketing campaigns. This competition drives continuous improvement and customer-focused strategies.

Example 2: In the airline industry, airlines compete for passengers by offering different fare options, in-flight amenities, or loyalty programmes. This competition encourages airlines to enhance their services and improve customer experiences.

E: External Influences at Play

Market dynamics are also affected by external factors beyond the control of individual businesses. Economic conditions, government regulations, technological advancements, and social trends can all impact how a market operates. Being aware of these external factors helps businesses anticipate changes and adapt their strategies accordingly.

Example 1: Government regulations on carbon emissions can significantly impact the automotive industry. Stricter regulations may require manufacturers to invest in electric or hybrid vehicles, driving innovation and changes in production processes.

Example 2: Technological advancements, such as the rise of e-commerce, have transformed the retail industry. Traditional brick-and-mortar retailers have had to adapt their strategies to compete with online retailers and provide seamless online shopping experiences.

F: Mastering the Supply Chain

Supply chain refers to the entire process involved in delivering a product or service from the supplier to the end consumer. It encompasses all the activities, organisations, resources, and information required to transform raw materials into finished products and deliver them to customers.

The supply chain typically consists of several interconnected stages or functions, each playing a crucial role in the overall process. Here is a detailed explanation of the key components of a supply chain:

1. **Procurement:** This involves sourcing and purchasing raw materials, components, or services needed for production. It includes activities such as supplier selection, negotiation, and contract management.
2. **Production:** This stage involves converting raw materials into finished products. It includes manufacturing processes, quality control, and managing production schedules to meet customer demand.
3. **Inventory Management:** This function deals with the storage, tracking, and control of inventory levels. It aims to strike a balance between ensuring product availability to meet customer demand while minimising carrying costs and stockouts.
4. Warehousing: Warehousing involves the physical storage of products before they are distributed to customers. It includes activities such as receiving, storing, picking, packing, and shipping goods.
5. **Transportation:** This component focuses on the movement of goods from one location to another. It includes selecting appropriate transportation

modes (such as trucks, ships, or planes), managing logistics providers, and optimising transportation routes.

6. **Distribution:** Distribution involves the final delivery of products to customers or retail outlets. It includes activities such as order fulfilment, order tracking, and managing customer returns.
7. **Demand Planning and Forecasting:** This function involves estimating future customer demand to ensure that the supply chain is adequately prepared. It includes analysing historical data, market trends, and customer behaviour to generate accurate demand forecasts.
8. **Supplier Relationship Management:** This aspect focuses on building and maintaining strong relationships with suppliers. It includes activities such as supplier performance evaluation, collaboration, and continuous improvement initiatives.
9. **Information Systems:** Information technology plays a vital role in supply chain management. It includes the use of systems such as Enterprise Resource Planning (ERP) software, inventory management systems, and data analytics tools to monitor and optimise various supply chain activities.
10. **Sustainability and Ethical Practices:** Increasingly, supply chains are incorporating sustainable and ethical practices. This includes considerations such as reducing carbon footprint, ensuring fair labour practices, responsible sourcing, and minimising waste.

Effective supply chain management requires coordination, collaboration, and synchronisation among all these components. It aims to ensure the right product, at the right quantity, reaches the right place, and at the right time while minimising costs and maximising customer satisfaction.

By managing the supply chain effectively, organizations can improve operational efficiency, reduce costs, enhance customer service, and gain a competitive advantage in the market.

In the context of market dynamics, the supply chain plays a crucial role in ensuring that products or services reach the market efficiently and effectively. Changes in the supply chain, such as disruptions in sourcing materials, transportation challenges, or delays in production, can impact market dynamics by affecting the availability and pricing of products. For example, if there is a shortage of raw materials due to supply chain disruptions, it can lead to higher prices and limited availability of certain products in the market.

G: Pivotal Partners: Key Vendors Explored

Key vendors are the suppliers or business partners that play a significant role in a company's supply chain. They provide essential goods, services, or components that are integral to the company's operations and the products or services it offers to customers.

In the realm of market dynamics, key vendors influence market conditions by their ability to meet the demands and requirements of businesses. The quality, reliability, pricing, and availability of the products or services supplied by key vendors can have a direct impact on a company's competitiveness, profitability, and customer satisfaction. Companies must carefully evaluate and select their key vendors to ensure smooth operations and maintain a competitive edge in the market.

H: Locational Advantages: The Power of Place

Locational advantage, also known as geographical advantage or location advantage, refers to the benefits or advantages that a business or organisation derives from its specific geographical location. It is a strategic factor that can impact the success and competitiveness of a company in the market.

Here is A More Detailed Explanation of Locational Advantage:

Access to Resources: One of the primary benefits of locational advantage is access to key resources. Different regions or locations may have abundant natural resources, such as raw materials, energy sources, or water supply, that are crucial for certain industries. Being situated close to these resources can provide cost advantages and ensure a stable supply chain.

Market Proximity: Locating a business in close proximity to its target market can offer significant advantages. It reduces transportation costs, allows for faster delivery times, and enhances customer responsiveness. Being near customers also facilitates a better understanding of their preferences, needs, and market trends, enabling companies to tailor their products or services accordingly.

Infrastructure and Logistics: Locational advantage often relates to the presence of well-developed infrastructure and logistics networks. Access to transportation systems, such as highways, ports, airports, or railways, can streamline the movement of goods and materials, reducing shipping costs and improving efficiency. Availability of robust communication networks and supportive business services can also enhance operational capabilities.

Labour Pool: The availability of a skilled and qualified workforce is critical for many businesses. Certain regions may have a larger pool of talent with expertise in specific industries or technologies. Locating in such areas allows companies to tap into a skilled labour force, reducing recruitment and training costs, and fostering innovation and productivity.

Government Support and Incentives: Governments often offer incentives and support to attract businesses to particular locations. These incentives can include tax breaks, grants, subsidies, or favourable regulations. Taking advantage of these offerings can provide cost savings and other benefits, making the chosen location more economically attractive.

Competitive Advantage: Locational advantage can create a competitive edge over rivals. It can deter new entrants into the market by establishing barriers to entry based on location-specific factors. Additionally, being located in a cluster or hub of related businesses or industries can foster collaboration, knowledge sharing, and access to specialised suppliers, customers, or research institutions.

Image and Reputation: Some locations carry a positive image or reputation associated with certain industries or sectors. Establishing a presence in these areas can enhance brand perception and credibility, attracting customers, partners, and investors. It can also provide networking opportunities and exposure to industry events, conferences, and talent pools.

It is important to note that locational advantage can vary depending on the industry, business model, and specific circumstances. What may be advantageous for one company may not be as significant for another. Therefore, organisations need to carefully evaluate the factors relevant to their business and align their location strategy accordingly.

By strategically leveraging locational advantages, businesses can optimise their operations, reduce costs, access key resources, and gain a competitive edge in the market.

In the context of market dynamics, locational advantages can significantly impact a company's market position and competitiveness. Companies situated in strategic locations may have easier access to raw materials, efficient transportation, or a favourable business environment, giving them a competitive edge. For example, a manufacturing company located near a major port can benefit from lower shipping costs and faster delivery to customers, thereby influencing market dynamics by providing competitive pricing or faster order fulfilment.

Conclusion

Balancing Supply and Demand: Sustained success hinges on businesses adeptly aligning their supply with market demand, necessitating agility and strategic adaptation.

The Dance of Price Fluctuations: Pricing strategies must be dynamic, responding to market forces while maximising profitability, highlighting the importance of strategic pricing models.

Deciphering Consumer Behavior: Informed decisions arise from a deep comprehension of consumer preferences, urging businesses to invest in market research and consumer insights.

Triumphing Amidst Competition: Thriving in a competitive landscape requires differentiation, innovation, and continuous evolution to maintain a distinctive edge.

External Influences at Play: Businesses must navigate external macroeconomic factors with proactivity, adaptability, and resilience to mitigate uncertainties.

Mastering the Supply Chain: An efficient supply chain is pivotal for operational excellence, urging businesses to invest in technology, collaboration, and sustainability.

Pivotal Partners: Key Vendors Explored: Strategic partnerships with key vendors enhance reliability and flexibility, emphasising the importance of aligning partnerships with long-term goals.

Locational Advantages: The Power of Place: Geography plays a crucial role, and businesses can leverage locational advantages for logistical efficiency and improved market accessibility.

Collectively, this chapter advocates for a holistic understanding of market dynamics, urging businesses to embrace adaptability, innovation, strategic partnerships, and a keen awareness of external influences to thrive in the ever-evolving marketplace.

I: Effective Questions to Ask the Leaders

- How does the supply chain operate within our organisation? Can you explain the key stages and processes involved?
- What are the primary factors that influence supply and demand in our industry?
- How do we ensure a smooth flow of goods/services within our supply chain? Are there any challenges we face in this regard?
- Who are our key vendors or suppliers, and how do we maintain strong relationships with them?
- How have consumer insights helped us in deciding the pricing of our products/services?
- What parameters do we look for when analysing our competitors?
- What criteria do we use to select vendors? How do we evaluate their performance and ensure quality control?
- Are there any specific strategies or initiatives in place to optimise our supply chain and reduce costs?
- How do we manage inventory levels to meet customer demand while minimising excess stock or shortages?
- Can you provide insights into any recent market trends or shifts in consumer preferences that may impact our supply chain?
- What measures do we take to mitigate risks related to supply chain disruptions, such as natural disasters or geopolitical events?
- How do we ensure ethical and sustainable practices throughout our supply chain?
- What role does our location play in giving us a competitive advantage? Are there any specific factors that make our location favourable for business operations?

- How do we leverage our local advantage to reach target markets more effectively?
- Are there any infrastructure or logistical challenges associated with our location that we need to address?
- Can you provide examples of how our local advantage has contributed to our competitive position in the market?
- How do we identify and select key vendors or partners who align with our business goals and values?
- What criteria do we use to evaluate the performance and reliability of our key vendors?
- How do we foster collaborative relationships with key vendors to drive mutual success?
- Are there any alternative vendors or suppliers we are considering to diversify our supply chain and mitigate risks?
- How do we stay updated on market trends and changes in consumer demand to adapt our supply chain and vendor strategies accordingly?
- Can you provide insights into any ongoing or planned initiatives to enhance our supply chain efficiency and strengthen relationships with key vendors?

Chapter IV

Roles and Departments: A Symbiotic Perspective

Why this Chapter?

In summary, understanding departments within an organisation is a key factor in making informed career decisions, planning your skill development, and maximising growth opportunities. It equips you with the insights needed to excel in your current role, advance within your chosen department, or make strategic transitions to new departments when necessary.

Informed Career Choices: Understanding different departments within an organisation allows you to make informed decisions about your career path. By knowing the functions and goals of each department, you can align your skills, interests, and career goals with the roles that offer the most growth potential.

Targeted Skill Development: Each department has its own set of skills that are valued and required for success. Having knowledge of these skills helps you focus on targeted skill development. This way, you can work on acquiring the abilities that are in demand within your chosen department, thus increasing your chances of advancement.

Identifying Growth Trajectories: Not all departments offer the same growth trajectories. Some departments might have a clear path to managerial roles, while others might emphasise specialised expertise. Understanding the growth opportunities within each department helps you plan your career journey and set realistic expectations for advancement.

Navigating Responsibilities: Knowing the responsibilities associated with different departments provides clarity on what will be expected of you in various roles. This knowledge can help you prepare for your current role and anticipate the skills and experience you need to develop for future roles.

Higher Education Choices: When considering higher education options, understanding the requirements of your desired department is crucial.

Certain roles might require specific degrees, certifications, or advanced education. Knowing these requirements can help you make informed decisions about pursuing further education.

Switching Departments Strategically: If you're considering switching departments within your organisation, knowing the differences in responsibilities, skills, and growth prospects can help you make a strategic move. You can leverage your existing skills and experiences while also learning new ones that are valued in the new department.

Enhancing Cross-Functional Collaboration: Knowledge of other departments promotes better collaboration and communication within the organisation. When you understand the roles and challenges of different teams, you can work more effectively on cross-functional projects and initiatives.

Adaptation to Organisational Changes: Organisations are dynamic, and they may undergo changes over time. Being knowledgeable about various departments allows you to adapt to changes such as restructures, new projects, or evolving business priorities more effectively.

A: Inside the World of Human Resources

The HR department plays a crucial role in organisations by managing the most valuable asset: the employees. It is responsible for various functions related to attracting, developing, and retaining a skilled and motivated workforce. Within the HR department, there are different positions and roles that contribute to the overall success of the department and the organisation as a whole.

HR Manager: The HR Manager is responsible for overseeing the entire HR department and developing strategic initiatives aligned with the organisation's goals. They establish HR policies and procedures, manage employee relations, and ensure legal compliance. They also collaborate with other departments to address HR needs and drive organisational culture.

Recruitment Specialist: The Recruitment Specialist focuses on attracting and selecting qualified candidates for open positions within the organisation. They develop recruitment strategies, create job postings, screen resumes, conduct interviews, and manage the onboarding process. They play a critical role in ensuring the organisation has the right talent to meet its objectives.

Training and Development Specialist: The Training and Development Specialist is responsible for assessing training needs, designing and delivering training programs, and evaluating their effectiveness. They identify skill gaps, develop training materials, and provide opportunities for employee development. Their role helps enhance employee performance and promote professional growth.

Compensation and Benefits Specialist: The Compensation and Benefits Specialist manages the organisation's compensation and benefits programs. They conduct salary research, develop pay structures, administer employee benefits, and ensure compliance with compensation regulations. Their role ensures fair and competitive compensation practices to attract and retain talented employees.

Employee Relations Specialist: The Employee Relations Specialist focuses on maintaining positive relationships between employees and the organisation. They address employee grievances, mediate conflicts, and promote a healthy work environment. They also enforce policies and procedures, provide guidance on employment regulations, and foster a culture of open communication.

HR Business Partner: The HR Business Partner works closely with business leaders and managers to align HR strategies with organisational goals. They serve as a consultant, providing guidance on talent management, performance management, and employee development. They act as a bridge between employees and management, ensuring HR initiatives support the overall business objectives.

HR Analyst: The HR Analyst collects and analyses HR data to identify trends, measure performance, and provide insights for decision-making. They create reports, develop HR metrics, and utilise data to support HR strategies and initiatives. Their role helps drive evidence-based HR practices and enhances the effectiveness of HR programs.

By understanding the different positions within the HR department and their roles and responsibilities, employees can gain visibility into their career growth opportunities. They can identify the skills, knowledge, and experiences required for each position and chart a clear career path within the HR field. Additionally, this understanding helps employees appreciate the diverse functions of the HR department and the importance of their contributions in attracting, developing, and retaining a talented workforce.

B: Decoding Financial and Accounting Functions

The Finance and Accounting department is a crucial component of any organisation as it is responsible for managing financial resources, tracking transactions, ensuring compliance with financial regulations, and providing accurate financial information for decision-making. Within this department, there are various positions with distinct roles and responsibilities, each contributing to the smooth functioning of the department and the financial health of the organisation.

Chief Financial Officer (CFO): The CFO is the senior-most position in the finance department and holds overall responsibility for the organisation's financial management. They develop financial strategies, oversee budgeting and forecasting, manage financial risks, and provide financial insights to support strategic decision-making. The CFO collaborates with other departments to align financial goals with the organisation's objectives.

Financial Controller: The Financial Controller is responsible for maintaining accurate and up-to-date financial records. They oversee accounting operations, financial reporting, and compliance with accounting standards and regulations. The Financial Controller also manages internal controls, audits, and financial analysis to ensure the organisation's financial integrity.

Financial Analyst: Financial Analysts analyze financial data and provide insights to support decision-making. They assess financial performance, conduct financial forecasting and modeling, and evaluate investment opportunities. Financial Analysts play a crucial role in providing recommendations for budgeting, cost control, and revenue optimization.

Accounts Payable (AP) Specialist: AP Specialists manage the payment processes and relationships with vendors and suppliers. They review and process invoices, reconcile accounts payable, and ensure timely and accurate payments. AP Specialists also handle vendor inquiries, resolve payment discrepancies, and maintain vendor records.

Accounts Receivable (AR) Specialist: AR Specialists are responsible for managing customer billing and collections. They prepare and send invoices, monitor customer payments, and follow up on outstanding receivables. AR Specialists also handle customer inquiries, resolve billing disputes, and maintain accurate customer records.

Tax Specialist: Tax Specialists handle tax-related matters for the organisation, ensuring compliance with tax laws and regulations. They prepare and file tax returns, conduct tax planning, and provide guidance on tax implications for business decisions. Tax Specialists stay updated on tax laws and changes to optimise tax strategies and minimise tax liabilities.

Financial Planning and Analysis (FP&A) Manager: FP&A Managers focus on financial planning, budgeting, and forecasting. They collaborate with various departments to develop budgets, monitor financial performance, and provide insights into financial trends and projections. FP&A Managers play a vital role in aligning financial goals with strategic objectives and driving financial accountability.

By understanding the different positions within the Finance and Accounting department and their roles and responsibilities, employees can gain visibility into their career growth opportunities. They can identify the skills, knowledge, and experiences required for each position and plan their career path within the finance field. This understanding also helps employees appreciate the importance of their contributions to maintaining financial integrity, supporting decision-making processes, and ensuring the organisation's financial health.

C: Science of Marketing

The Marketing department plays a critical role in promoting a company's products or services, building brand awareness, and driving customer engagement. It encompasses various positions, each with unique responsibilities that contribute to the overall marketing strategy and success of the organisation. Understanding these positions can provide employees with visibility into their career growth opportunities and help them grasp the diverse range of work and responsibilities within the marketing field.

Marketing Manager: Marketing Managers are responsible for developing and implementing marketing strategies to achieve business objectives. They oversee the marketing team, conduct market research, analyze consumer behaviour, and identify target markets. Marketing Managers collaborate with other departments to align marketing efforts with overall business goals and monitor the success of marketing campaigns.

Brand Manager: Brand Managers focus on managing and enhancing the company's brand image. They develop brand strategies, create brand guidelines, and ensure consistent brand messaging across all marketing channels. Brand Managers work closely with the creative team to develop compelling brand visuals and messaging that resonate with the target audience.

Digital Marketing Specialist: Digital Marketing Specialists are experts in online marketing channels such as search engine optimisation (SEO), social media marketing, email marketing, and content marketing. They create and execute digital marketing campaigns, monitor website traffic and engagement, and optimise online marketing activities to drive customer acquisition and engagement.

Advertising Manager: Advertising Managers oversee the planning and execution of advertising campaigns across various media channels. They work with creative agencies to develop impactful ad creatives, negotiate advertising contracts, and analyse the effectiveness of advertising campaigns. Advertising Managers ensure that advertising efforts align with the overall marketing strategy and brand messaging.

Market Research Analyst: Market Research Analysts gather and analyse data to identify market trends, consumer preferences, and competitive landscape. They conduct surveys, interviews, and analyse market data to provide insights for product development, pricing strategies, and market segmentation. Market Research Analysts help the marketing team make data-driven decisions and stay ahead of market changes.

Social Media Manager: Social Media Managers are responsible for managing the company's presence on social media platforms. They develop social media strategies, create engaging content, and monitor social media channels for customer engagement and feedback. Social Media Managers also analyse social media metrics to measure the impact of social media efforts and identify areas for improvement.

Public Relations (PR) Specialist: PR Specialists manage the company's public image and handle relationships with the media. They develop PR strategies, write press releases, organise media events, and manage crisis communications. PR Specialists help build positive brand reputation, handle media inquiries, and ensure consistent messaging across various communication channels.

Understanding the roles and responsibilities within the Marketing department can provide employees with a clear career progression path. It helps them identify the specific skills, knowledge, and experiences required for each position and allows them to set goals and develop their expertise accordingly. By gaining visibility into their career graph, employees can align their efforts and responsibilities with the broader marketing strategy, contribute to the success of marketing campaigns, and pursue growth opportunities within the dynamic field of marketing.

D: Operations: Behind-the-Scenes Excellence

The Operations & Supply Chain department is a critical function within an organisation that ensures the efficient flow of goods, services, and information from suppliers to customers. It involves various positions, each with distinct responsibilities that contribute to the smooth operations and overall success of the company. Understanding the roles and responsibilities within this department can provide employees with visibility into their career growth opportunities and help them understand the diverse range of work and responsibilities involved in operations and supply chain management.

Operations Manager: Operations Managers oversee the entire operations function and are responsible for optimising the production processes, ensuring timely delivery of products or services, and maximising operational efficiency. They coordinate with different departments, set performance targets, manage resources, and implement strategies to improve productivity and quality.

Supply Chain Analyst: Supply Chain Analysts are responsible for analysing and optimising the supply chain operations. They analyse data, monitor inventory levels, identify bottlenecks, and suggest improvements to enhance efficiency and reduce costs. Supply Chain Analysts work closely with suppliers, logistics partners, and internal teams to ensure smooth coordination and timely delivery.

Procurement Manager: Procurement Managers are in charge of sourcing and procuring materials, products, or services required for the organisation's operations. They identify reliable suppliers, negotiate contracts, manage supplier relationships, and ensure that the procurement process is efficient and cost-effective. Procurement Managers also monitor market trends and make strategic decisions to optimise the procurement function.

Warehouse Manager: Warehouse Managers oversee the storage, organisation, and distribution of goods within the company's warehouses.

They ensure proper inventory management, implement efficient warehouse layouts, manage receiving and shipping processes, and optimise warehouse operations to meet customer demands while minimising costs.

Logistics Coordinator: Logistics Coordinators are responsible for coordinating the transportation and distribution of goods. They plan and schedule shipments, work with carriers and freight forwarders, track shipments, and address any logistics issues that may arise. Logistics Coordinators play a crucial role in ensuring the timely and efficient movement of products throughout the supply chain.

Quality Assurance Manager: Quality Assurance Managers are responsible for maintaining and improving the quality standards of products or services. They develop and implement quality control processes, conduct inspections and audits, analyse data to identify areas for improvement, and collaborate with cross-functional teams to enhance product or service quality.

Demand Planner: Demand Planners forecast customer demand for products or services based on historical data, market trends, and other factors. They collaborate with sales, marketing, and production teams to ensure accurate demand forecasts, optimise inventory levels, and minimise stock-outs or excess inventory. Demand Planners play a crucial role in balancing supply and demand to meet customer expectations.

Understanding the various roles within the Operations & Supply Chain department helps employees gain visibility into their career paths. It enables them to identify specific skills, knowledge, and experiences required for each role and empowers them to set goals and develop their expertise accordingly. By understanding their career graph, employees can align their efforts and responsibilities with the broader operations and supply chain strategy, contribute to operational excellence, and pursue growth opportunities within the field of operations and supply chain management.

E: Unveiling IT and Technology Endeavours

The IT & Technology department plays a critical role in modern organisations, driving innovation, managing digital infrastructure, and supporting the technology needs of the business. It encompasses various positions, each with distinct responsibilities, which contribute to the efficient functioning of the department and the overall success of the company. Understanding the roles and responsibilities within this department can provide employees with visibility into their career growth opportunities and help them understand the diverse range of work and responsibilities involved in IT and technology management.

IT Manager/Director: IT Managers or Directors oversee the entire IT department and are responsible for developing and implementing IT strategies aligned with business goals. They manage the department's budget, set priorities, and ensure that technology solutions are effectively deployed and maintained. They also collaborate with other departments to understand their technology needs and provide guidance on IT initiatives.

System Administrator: System Administrators are responsible for managing the company's computer systems, servers, and networks. They configure and maintain hardware and software, troubleshoot technical issues, and ensure the security and integrity of the IT infrastructure. System Administrators also perform regular system backups, monitor system performance, and implement upgrades or patches as needed.

Network Engineer: Network Engineers design, implement, and manage the organisation's computer networks. They configure routers, switches, and firewalls, monitor network performance, troubleshoot connectivity issues, and ensure network security. Network Engineers also collaborate with other teams to design and implement network upgrades or expansions to meet the organisation's evolving needs.

Software Developer/Engineer: Software Developers or Engineers design, develop, and maintain software applications and systems used within the organisation. They collaborate with stakeholders to understand requirements, write code, conduct testing, and ensure the quality and functionality of the software. Software Developers/Engineers also stay updated with the latest technology trends and best practices to drive innovation in software development.

Database Administrator: Database Administrators manage the organisation's databases, ensuring data integrity, security, and availability. They design and optimise database structures, implement backup and recovery procedures, monitor database performance, and troubleshoot any issues that may arise. Database Administrators also work closely with other teams to ensure data integration and support data-driven decision-making.

IT Support Specialist: IT Support Specialists provide technical assistance and support to users within the organisation. They help troubleshoot hardware or software issues, install and configure computer systems, provide training to users, and maintain documentation of IT procedures. IT Support Specialists play a crucial role in ensuring that employees can effectively use technology tools to perform their roles.

IT Project Manager: IT Project Managers oversee the planning, execution, and monitoring of IT projects within the organisation. They define project scope, allocate resources, manage timelines and budgets, and ensure that projects are delivered successfully. IT Project Managers collaborate with cross-functional teams, communicate project status, and mitigate risks to ensure the timely completion of IT initiatives.

Understanding the various roles within the IT & Technology department helps employees gain visibility into their career paths. It enables them to identify specific skills, knowledge, and experiences required for each role and empowers them to set goals and develop their expertise accordingly. By understanding their career graph, employees can align their efforts and responsibilities with the broader IT and technology strategy, contribute to technological advancements within the organisation, and pursue growth opportunities within the field of IT and technology management.

F: Engineering and Production Dance

The Engineering and Production department is a critical component of any organisation involved in manufacturing or product development. It encompasses various roles and positions, each with distinct responsibilities, which collectively contribute to the efficient design, development, and production of goods. Understanding the roles and responsibilities within this department can provide employees with visibility into their career growth opportunities and help them understand the diverse range of work and responsibilities involved in engineering and production management.

Engineering Manager/Director: Engineering Managers or Directors oversee the engineering department and are responsible for managing engineering projects, setting goals and objectives, and ensuring the timely and successful completion of projects. They coordinate with cross-functional teams, collaborate with stakeholders, and provide guidance and leadership to engineers to ensure the delivery of high-quality products or projects.

Design Engineer: Design Engineers are responsible for creating and developing product designs. They collaborate with stakeholders to understand requirements, conduct research, and use computer-aided design (CAD) software to create detailed product drawings and specifications. Design Engineers consider factors such as functionality, aesthetics, manufacturability, and cost-effectiveness to develop innovative and feasible product designs.

Manufacturing Engineer: Manufacturing Engineers focus on optimising the production process and ensuring efficient manufacturing operations. They analyse production methods, identify areas for improvement, and implement strategies to enhance productivity, reduce costs, and improve quality. Manufacturing Engineers work closely with production teams, evaluate equipment and machinery, and develop and implement manufacturing processes and procedures.

Quality Control/Assurance Engineer: Quality Control or Assurance Engineers play a crucial role in ensuring that products meet the required quality standards. They develop and implement quality control processes, conduct inspections and tests, analyse data, and identify and resolve quality issues. Quality Control/Assurance Engineers work closely with design and production teams to implement quality improvements and ensure customer satisfaction.

Process Engineer: Process Engineers focus on optimising production processes and workflows. They analyse existing processes, identify bottlenecks or inefficiencies, and develop and implement improvements. Process Engineers may use tools such as Six Sigma or Lean methodologies to streamline operations, reduce waste, and increase efficiency. They collaborate with cross-functional teams to implement process changes and monitor their effectiveness.

Production Supervisor/Manager: Production Supervisors or Managers are responsible for overseeing the day-to-day operations of the production floor. They manage production schedules, allocate resources, monitor production output, and ensure adherence to quality and safety standards. Production Supervisors/Managers also provide leadership and guidance to production teams, address any issues or challenges that arise, and drive continuous improvement in production processes.

Test Engineer: Test Engineers are involved in testing and validating products to ensure they meet the required specifications and performance standards. They develop test plans, conduct tests, analyse data, and troubleshoot any issues that may arise. Test Engineers work closely with design and production teams to verify product functionality, identify areas for improvement, and ensure product reliability.

Understanding the various roles within the Engineering and Production department helps employees gain visibility into their career paths. It enables them to identify specific skills, knowledge, and experiences required for each role and empowers them to set goals and develop their expertise accordingly. By understanding their career graph, employees can align their efforts and responsibilities with the broader engineering and production strategy, contribute to product development and manufacturing excellence, and pursue growth opportunities within the field of engineering and production management.

G: Innovators Unleashed: Research and Development

The Research and Development (R&D) department plays a crucial role in driving innovation, creating new products or services, and enhancing existing offerings within an organisation. It is responsible for conducting research, exploring new technologies, and developing cutting-edge solutions to meet customer needs and stay ahead of the competition. Understanding the roles and responsibilities within the R&D department can provide employees with visibility into their career growth opportunities and help them understand the diverse range of work and responsibilities involved in research and development.

Research Scientist: Research Scientists are responsible for conducting scientific investigations, exploring new ideas, and developing new technologies or methodologies. They design and execute experiments, analyse data, and contribute to the development of innovative products or solutions. Research Scientists stay up-to-date with the latest advancements in their field and collaborate with cross-functional teams to translate research findings into practical applications.

Product Development Engineer: Product Development Engineers are involved in the design and development of new products or improvements to existing ones. They work closely with stakeholders to understand customer requirements, conduct feasibility studies, and create prototypes. Product Development Engineers consider factors such as functionality, cost, and manufacturability, ensuring that the final product meets customer needs and aligns with the organisation's goals.

Project Manager: Project Managers in the R&D department are responsible for overseeing and coordinating research projects. They develop project plans, allocate resources, set timelines, and ensure that projects are delivered on time and within budget. Project Managers also collaborate with stakeholders, facilitate communication, and manage risks and challenges throughout the project lifecycle.

Technical Writer: Technical Writers play a vital role in documenting research findings, creating user manuals, and writing technical reports. They translate complex scientific or technical information into clear and concise language, making it accessible to both internal teams and external stakeholders. Technical Writers also collaborate with researchers and engineers to understand their work and effectively communicate it to different audiences.

Intellectual Property Specialist: Intellectual Property (IP) Specialists are responsible for protecting the organisation's innovations, inventions, and technologies. They conduct patent searches, prepare patent applications, and ensure compliance with intellectual property laws and regulations. IP Specialists also collaborate with legal teams to handle patent filings, infringement issues, and licensing agreements.

Data Analyst: Data Analysts in the R&D department analyse research data, conduct statistical analyses, and derive meaningful insights. They use various tools and techniques to interpret data, identify trends, and support decision-making processes. Data Analysts work closely with researchers and scientists to ensure that data is collected accurately and analyse the results to drive informed research outcomes.

Quality Assurance Specialist: Quality Assurance (QA) Specialists ensure that R&D processes and procedures adhere to quality standards. They develop quality control measures, conduct audits, and monitor compliance. QA Specialists collaborate with cross-functional teams to implement quality improvement initiatives, address quality-related issues, and ensure that products or solutions meet regulatory requirements and customer expectations.

Understanding the various roles within the R&D department helps employees gain visibility into their career paths. It enables them to identify specific skills, knowledge, and experiences required for each role and empowers them to set goals and develop their expertise accordingly. By understanding their career graph, employees can align their efforts and responsibilities with the broader R&D strategy, contribute to innovation and product development, and pursue growth opportunities within the field of research and development.

H: The Legal Frontier

The Legal department within an organisation plays a critical role in ensuring legal compliance, managing risks, and providing legal guidance and support. Understanding the various positions within the Legal department can help employees gain visibility into their career growth opportunities and comprehend the different types of work and responsibilities involved in the legal profession.

General Counsel: The General Counsel is the head of the Legal department and holds a senior leadership position. They are responsible for overseeing all legal matters within the organisation, providing strategic legal advice to senior management, and managing the legal team. The General Counsel plays a crucial role in setting the legal direction and ensuring that the organisation operates within the boundaries of the law.

Corporate Counsel: Corporate Counsel, also known as In-House Counsel, are lawyers who work directly within the organisation. They handle a wide range of legal issues specific to the business, including contract drafting and negotiation, intellectual property matters, employment law compliance, regulatory compliance, and corporate governance. Corporate Counsel act as legal advisors to internal stakeholders, offering guidance on legal risks and strategies.

Compliance Officer: Compliance Officers are responsible for ensuring that the organisation adheres to relevant laws, regulations, and internal policies. They develop and implement compliance programs, conduct risk assessments, provide training to employees, and monitor compliance activities. Compliance Officers play a crucial role in mitigating legal and regulatory risks, promoting ethical behaviour, and maintaining the organisation's reputation.

Contracts Manager: Contracts Managers are responsible for the management and administration of contracts within the organisation. They review, negotiate, and draft various types of contracts, such as vendor agreements, client contracts, and partnership agreements. Contracts Managers ensure that contracts are legally sound, protect the organisation's interests, and comply with applicable laws and regulations.

Intellectual Property (IP) Attorney: IP Attorneys specialise in protecting the organisation's intellectual property rights, including trademarks, copyrights, and patents. They handle the registration and enforcement of IP assets, conduct IP searches, and provide guidance on IP strategies. IP Attorneys also assist in drafting licensing agreements, resolving IP disputes, and ensuring the organisation's intellectual property is safeguarded.

Litigation Counsel: Litigation Counsel represent the organisation in legal disputes, whether as plaintiffs or defendants. They handle litigation matters, including court appearances, legal research, document preparation, and negotiations. Litigation Counsel work closely with external law firms, manage legal budgets, and strategise to protect the organisation's interests during legal proceedings.

Legal Analyst: Legal Analysts provide support to the legal team by conducting legal research, analysing statutes and regulations, and preparing legal documents and briefs. They assist in legal due diligence, contract reviews, and analysing the impact of new laws or regulations on the organisation. Legal Analysts play a vital role in providing accurate and timely legal information to support decision-making processes.

Understanding the roles and responsibilities within the Legal department allows employees to map out their career paths in the legal profession. It helps them identify areas of interest, develop specific legal skills, and pursue growth opportunities within the organisation. By gaining visibility into their career graphs, employees can work towards becoming legal experts in their chosen fields, contribute to risk management and compliance efforts, and support the organisation's overall legal strategy and objectives.

I: Science of Selling: Exploring Sales

The Sales department is a critical function within an organisation, responsible for driving revenue and achieving sales targets. Understanding the various positions within the Sales department can provide employees with visibility into their career growth opportunities and help them understand the different roles and responsibilities involved in sales.

Sales Representative: Sales Representatives are the front-line employees who directly engage with customers. Their primary responsibility is to generate sales by prospecting, qualifying leads, and closing deals. They build relationships with customers, understand their needs, and present product or service offerings. Sales Representatives play a crucial role in achieving sales targets and meeting customer expectations.

Key Account Manager: Key Account Managers are responsible for managing relationships with key clients or accounts. They work closely with strategic customers, understand their business objectives, and develop customised solutions to meet their needs. Key Account Managers focus on nurturing long-term relationships, identifying growth opportunities, and ensuring customer satisfaction. They play a vital role in maximising revenue from key accounts.

Sales Manager: Sales Managers oversee the sales team and are responsible for setting sales targets, developing sales strategies, and driving team performance. They provide guidance and support to Sales Representatives, monitor sales activities, and analyse sales data to identify trends and opportunities. Sales Managers also collaborate with other departments to align sales efforts with overall business objectives.

Sales Operations Manager: Sales Operations Managers handle the operational aspects of the sales function. They manage sales processes, systems, and tools to enhance efficiency and effectiveness. Sales Operations Managers analyse sales data, generate reports, and provide insights to support decision-making. They also coordinate sales training, territory planning, and incentive programs to optimise sales performance.

Sales Enablement Specialist: Sales Enablement Specialists support the sales team by providing them with the tools, resources, and training needed to succeed. They develop sales collateral, sales presentations, and product or service information. Sales Enablement Specialists also conduct sales training sessions and provide ongoing coaching to enhance the sales team's knowledge and skills.

Sales Analyst: Sales Analysts analyse sales data, market trends, and customer insights to support sales strategies and decision-making. They identify opportunities for sales growth, evaluate sales performance, and forecast future sales. Sales Analysts provide valuable insights to Sales Managers and other stakeholders to optimise sales strategies and improve sales effectiveness.

Sales Operations Coordinator: Sales Operations Coordinators provide administrative support to the sales team. They assist with order processing, inventory management, and sales documentation. Sales Operations Coordinators ensure smooth coordination between the sales team and other departments, such as finance, logistics, and customer service, to ensure timely and accurate order fulfilment.

Understanding the roles and responsibilities within the Sales department helps employees navigate their career paths in sales. It allows them to develop expertise in specific areas, such as account management, sales strategy, or sales operations. By gaining visibility into their career graphs, employees can work towards becoming sales leaders, expanding their networks, and contributing to the organisation's sales growth and success.

J: Organisational Backbone: Administrative Excellence

The Administrative department is a crucial function within an organisation that supports the smooth operation of various business activities. Employees working in different positions within the Administrative department play essential roles and hold responsibilities that contribute to the overall efficiency and effectiveness of the organisation.

Administrative Assistant: Administrative Assistants provide administrative support to various departments and individuals within the organisation. They manage schedules, coordinate meetings, handle correspondence, and perform general office tasks. Administrative Assistants often serve as the first point of contact for external stakeholders and internal staff, ensuring effective communication and maintaining a professional and organised office environment.

Office Manager: Office Managers oversee the day-to-day operations of the office and ensure its efficient functioning. They manage administrative staff, allocate resources, and implement policies and procedures to streamline workflows. Office Managers also handle budgeting, procurement of office supplies, and facility management. They play a vital role in creating a productive and well-organised work environment for employees.

Receptionist: Receptionists are responsible for managing incoming calls, greeting visitors, and directing them to the appropriate individuals or departments. They provide general information about the organisation, handle inquiries, and maintain a welcoming atmosphere in the reception area. Receptionists often serve as the first point of contact for clients, customers, and other stakeholders, making a positive first impression on behalf of the organisation.

Data Entry Specialist: Data Entry Specialists are responsible for accurately entering and maintaining data in the organisation's systems or databases. They ensure data integrity, perform data validation, and update records as required. Data Entry Specialists play a critical role in maintaining accurate and up-to-date information, which is essential for effective decision-making and efficient business processes.

Executive Assistant: Executive Assistants provide high-level administrative support to executives or senior management within the organisation. They handle sensitive and confidential information, manage calendars, coordinate travel arrangements, and assist with various administrative tasks. Executive Assistants often act as a gatekeeper for executives, managing their correspondence and facilitating communication with internal and external stakeholders.

Records Management Specialist: Records Management Specialists are responsible for organising and maintaining the organisation's records and documents. They develop and implement records management systems, ensure compliance with legal and regulatory requirements, and oversee the retention and disposal of records. Records Management Specialists play a crucial role in efficient document management, ensuring information is accessible, secure, and well-organised.

HR Coordinator: HR Coordinators support the Human Resources department by assisting with various HR functions. They may assist with recruitment and onboarding processes, maintain employee records, coordinate training and development programs, and handle HR-related documentation. HR Coordinators contribute to the smooth functioning of HR processes, supporting the organisation's talent management and employee engagement initiatives.

Understanding the various positions within the Administrative department helps employees gain visibility into their career paths and opportunities for growth. As employees progress in their careers, they can take on more significant responsibilities, such as managing teams, overseeing office operations, or specialising in specific areas like records management or HR. By demonstrating competence, professionalism, and a strong work ethic, employees in the Administrative department can advance their careers and contribute to the overall success of the organisation.

Conclusion

"Inside the World of Human Resources" unveils the pivotal role HR and its job profiles play in organisational dynamics. Recognising employees as valuable assets, this section emphasises fostering a positive work culture, talent acquisition, and employee development for overall organisational success.

"Decoding Financial and Accounting Functions" provides insights into the critical role finance and its job profile plays. Understanding financial intricacies empowers businesses to make informed decisions, manage resources efficiently, and ensure financial sustainability.

"Science of Marketing" delves into the art and science of customer engagement and their job profiles. Recognising marketing as a strategic driver, businesses are urged to embrace data-driven approaches, market research, and innovative campaigns for effective brand positioning.

"Operations: Behind-the-Scenes Excellence" highlights the unsung heroes and their job profiles ensuring seamless business processes. This section emphasises the significance of optimising operational efficiency, supply chain management, and quality control for overall organisational success.

"Unveiling IT and Technology Endeavors" explores the transformative role of technology and its job profiles. Acknowledging IT as a strategic enabler, businesses are encouraged to embrace innovation, cybersecurity, and digital transformation for a competitive edge.

"Engineering and Production Dance" sheds light on the synergy between design, production and their job profiles. Recognising the importance of seamless collaboration, businesses are prompted to integrate engineering and production processes for efficient and high-quality output.

"Innovators Unleashed: Research and Development" underscores the significance of R&D in driving innovation and their job profiles. This section encourages research, experimentation, and a culture of curiosity to stay at the forefront of industry advancements.

"The Legal Frontier" navigates the legal landscape impacting business and their job profiles. Recognising legal considerations as integral, businesses are urged to prioritise compliance, risk management, and ethical practices to safeguard their interests.

"Science of Selling: Exploring Sales" delves into the art of selling and their job profiles. Acknowledging sales as a dynamic process, businesses are prompted to understand customer needs, employ effective communication, and build lasting relationships for sustainable success.

"Organisational Backbone: Administrative Excellence" recognises the foundational role of administrative functions and their job profiles. Businesses are encouraged to prioritise organisational efficiency, effective communication, and streamlined processes to maintain a strong and agile backbone.

In essence, this chapter advocates for a symbiotic view of roles and departments, emphasising the interconnectedness of diverse functions for holistic organisational success. Each job role contributes uniquely to the organisational tapestry, and an appreciation of these symbiotic relationships fosters a more cohesive and effective working environment.

K: Effective Questions to Ask the Leaders

- What are the key responsibilities of the HR department in the company?
- How does the HR department handle recruitment and talent acquisition?
- Can you explain the employee onboarding and orientation process?
- How does the HR department support employee training and development?
- What performance management systems are in place for employee evaluations and promotions?

- How does the HR department handle employee relations and conflict resolution?
- Can you explain the company's compensation and benefits structure?
- What policies and procedures does the HR department oversee?
- Are there opportunities for career growth within the HR department?
- Can you provide examples of how the HR department has contributed to the company's success?
- What are the main responsibilities of the finance and accounting department?
- How does the department handle financial planning, budgeting, and forecasting?
- Can you explain the company's financial reporting and analysis processes?
- How does the department manage cash flow and financial risk?
- What role does the finance and accounting department play in tax planning and compliance?
- Can you provide an overview of the company's financial policies and procedures?
- How does the department collaborate with other departments to support their financial needs?
- Are there opportunities for career growth within the finance and accounting department?
- Can you share examples of how the finance and accounting department has contributed to the company's growth and success?
- What software or tools does the department use for financial management and reporting?
- What are the main objectives and goals of the marketing department?
- Can you explain the company's overall marketing strategy and target market?
- How does the marketing department conduct market research and analyse consumer behaviour?

- What channels and tactics does the department use for advertising and promotion?
- Can you provide examples of successful marketing campaigns the company has implemented?
- How does the marketing department measure the effectiveness of its efforts and track return on investment (ROI)?
- How does the department collaborate with sales and other departments to achieve marketing objectives?
- Are there opportunities for career growth within the marketing department?
- Can you share insights on upcoming marketing initiatives or projects the department is working on?
- How does the marketing department contribute to the company's overall growth and success?
- What are the main responsibilities of the operations department?
- Can you explain the company's supply chain management and logistics processes?
- How does the department ensure efficient production and delivery of goods or services?
- What measures does the department take to ensure quality control and process improvement?
- Can you provide an overview of the company's inventory management and procurement procedures?
- How does the operations department monitor and optimise operational costs?
- How does the department ensure compliance with relevant regulations and standards?
- Are there opportunities for career growth within the operations department?
- Can you share examples of how the operations department has contributed to improving productivity or reducing costs?
- How does the operations department collaborate with other departments to achieve organisational goals?

- What are the main responsibilities of the IT & Technology department?
- Can you provide an overview of the company's technology infrastructure and systems?
- How does the department handle network security and data protection?
- What software and tools does the department use to support the company's operations?
- Can you explain the IT department's role in system implementation and maintenance?
- How does the department handle IT support and troubleshooting for employees?
- Can you provide insights on any ongoing technology projects or initiatives?
- How does the IT department collaborate with other departments to meet their technology needs?
- What are the main responsibilities of the engineering and production department?
- Can you explain the product development and design process within the department?
- How does the department ensure efficient manufacturing and production processes?
- What quality control measures are in place to ensure product excellence?
- Can you provide examples of any successful engineering or production projects the department has completed?
- How does the department collaborate with other departments, such as R&D and operations?
- Are there opportunities for career growth within the engineering and production department?
- Can you share insights on any upcoming engineering or production initiatives or advancements?
- How does the department contribute to cost optimisation and process improvement?

- What safety protocols and regulations does the department follow to ensure a safe working environment?
- What are the main responsibilities of the research and development (R&D) department?
- Can you explain the R&D process and how new ideas or innovations are developed?
- How does the department collaborate with other departments, such as engineering and marketing?
- Can you provide examples of successful R&D projects or product innovations?
- How does the department stay updated on industry trends and advancements?
- What role does the department play in intellectual property protection and patent filing?
- Are there opportunities for career growth within the R&D department?
- Can you share insights on any ongoing R&D projects or initiatives?
- How does the R&D department contribute to the company's competitive advantage and growth?
- What resources and technologies does the department use for research and development activities?
- What are the main responsibilities of the legal department?
- Can you explain the department's role in contract management and legal compliance?
- How does the department handle legal disputes and litigation matters?
- What steps does the legal department take to protect the company's intellectual property?
- Can you provide insights on any recent or significant legal issues the department has addressed?
- How does the department support other departments in navigating legal and regulatory requirements?
- Are there opportunities for career growth within the legal department?

- Can you share examples of how the legal department has contributed to risk mitigation and ensuring legal compliance?
- How does the department stay updated on changes in laws and regulations relevant to the industry?
- What legal challenges or opportunities does the department foresee for the company in the near future?
- What are the main responsibilities of the sales department?
- Can you explain the sales process and how the department acquires and retains customers?
- How does the department set sales targets and develop sales strategies?
- What measures does the department take to analyse market trends and customer needs?
- Can you provide examples of successful sales campaigns or strategies the department has implemented?
- How does the department collaborate with marketing and other departments to drive sales?
- Are there opportunities for career growth within the sales department?
- Can you share insights on any upcoming sales initiatives or expansion plans?
- How does the sales department contribute to revenue generation and the company's overall growth?
- What sales training and development opportunities are provided to the sales team?
- What are the main responsibilities of the administrative department?
- Can you explain the department's role in managing office operations and administrative tasks?
- How does the department handle facilities management and maintenance?
- What measures are in place to ensure effective communication and coordination within the organisation?
- Can you provide examples of how the administrative department supports other departments?

- How does the department handle travel arrangements and event coordination?
- Are there opportunities for career growth within the administrative department?
- Can you share insights on any upcoming administrative projects or process improvements?
- How does the administrative department contribute to maintaining a positive work environment?
- What software or tools does the department use to streamline administrative tasks and processes?

Chapter V

Exploring Business Landscapes

Why this Chapter?

Understanding different types of business models and the distinction between products and services is like having a secret map for navigating your early career. You see, many folks don't realise how much the type of business affects the way it grows and operates. If you're not aware of this, it's easy to find yourself in a job that feels too fast or too slow for your pace. That's where learning about these things becomes a stress-busting superpower.

Think of it this way: different businesses are like different animals. Some can sprint and grow super fast, while others take it slow and steady. If you're someone who prefers a laid-back approach but ends up working in a super-fast-paced business, it's like forcing a turtle to race against a rabbit—it's not a happy situation. That's why it's important to understand the major types of businesses and their growth speeds so you can pick a job that matches your style and keeps stress at bay.

Here's the scoop: it's a good idea to dip your toes into different types of businesses early on in your career. It's like trying different flavours of ice cream to figure out your favourite. You might get lucky and find your perfect fit right away, but it's still smart to give a few options a shot. Sometimes, we get stuck thinking we know what's best for us, without giving other options a chance. You might think you're an 8/10 match for one company, but guess what? Another business might be a whopping 10/10 match for you—you'll never know until you give it a shot.

Let me share my own story. I personally thrive in companies that deal with products and grow quickly. So, landing in a snappy-paced B2B startup that focused on products was like finding a puzzle piece that fits just right. But let me tell you, it took me quite a few years and a bit of career hopping to figure that out.

So, dear learner, remember this: the type of business you work in is like the music that sets the tone for your career dance. Learning about different beats early on and trying out a few moves can save you from dancing to a tune that doesn't match your rhythm. So don't hesitate to explore, experiment, and groove your way to a career that fits you like your favourite pair of sneakers.

A: Decoding Business Types: B2B, B2C, and C2C Explained

B2B, or business-to-business, refers to transactions, interactions, and relationships between two or more businesses. In this context, one business is the supplier, while the other is the customer or client. B2B transactions typically involve the exchange of products, services, or information that support the operations of the purchasing business. Here is a detailed explanation of B2B along with three examples:

B2B Transactions: B2B transactions involve businesses purchasing goods or services from other businesses to support their own operations. These transactions can include raw materials, components, equipment, software solutions, professional services, and more. B2B transactions are often conducted through contractual agreements, purchase orders, or service-level agreements that define the terms, conditions, and specifications of the products or services being exchanged.

Example 1: A manufacturing company purchases steel, machinery, and other raw materials from various suppliers to produce its products. The company relies on B2B transactions to ensure a steady supply of quality materials for its manufacturing processes.

Example 2: An IT consulting firm partners with a software development company to provide customised software solutions for its clients. The consulting firm acts as the intermediary between the software development company and the clients, facilitating the B2B transaction and ensuring the delivery of tailored software products.

Example 3: A marketing agency collaborates with a printing company to produce marketing collateral such as brochures, flyers, and banners for their clients. The marketing agency relies on the printing company's expertise and resources to deliver high-quality printed materials for their B2B clients.

Relationship Building: B2B transactions often involve building long-term relationships between businesses. Trust, reliability, and mutual understanding are essential in B2B relationships. Both parties strive to establish strong connections based on the quality of products or services, timely delivery, effective communication, and responsiveness to changing needs.

Example 1: A construction company develops a long-term relationship with a cement supplier. Over time, they establish a trusted partnership based on the consistent supply of high-quality cement, on-time deliveries, competitive pricing, and open communication channels.

Example 2: An e-commerce platform forms strategic partnerships with various logistics companies to ensure efficient and reliable product delivery to its customers. The e-commerce platform values the logistics companies' ability to meet delivery timelines and handle the increasing volume of shipments.

Example 3: A software development company collaborates with a cloud hosting provider to ensure reliable and secure hosting services for its applications. The software development company values the provider's expertise in managing infrastructure and data security, which contributes to a long-term and trustworthy partnership.

B2B Marketing and Sales: B2B marketing and sales strategies focus on reaching and influencing key decision-makers within other businesses. B2B marketing often involves targeted campaigns, industry-specific advertising, trade shows, and digital marketing efforts. Sales teams engage in direct sales and negotiations with business clients, highlighting the unique value proposition, cost-effectiveness, and benefits of their products or services.

Example 1: A software company conducts targeted online marketing campaigns to reach IT managers and decision-makers in businesses, showcasing the features, benefits, and cost savings of their enterprise software solutions.

Example 2: A commercial cleaning services provider participates in industry-specific trade shows and exhibitions, where they can connect with facility managers and present their expertise, eco-friendly practices, and high-quality service offerings.

Example 3: A business consulting firm employs a dedicated sales team to engage with potential clients, understand their specific business needs, and pitch customised consulting solutions that can improve efficiency, productivity, and profitability.

In summary, B2B transactions involve businesses buying and selling goods or services to support their operations. Building strong relationships, effective marketing and sales strategies, and tailored solutions are key aspects of successful B2B interactions.

B2C, or business-to-consumer, refers to transactions, interactions, and relationships between a business and individual consumers. In B2C transactions, businesses sell products or services directly to consumers for personal use or consumption. B2C interactions typically occur through various channels, including physical retail stores, e-commerce platforms, mobile applications, and other direct-to-consumer channels. Here is a detailed explanation of B2C along with three examples:

B2C Transactions: B2C transactions involve businesses selling products or services directly to individual consumers. These transactions can range from everyday consumer goods, such as clothing, electronics, and groceries, to services like travel bookings, spa treatments, or online courses. B2C transactions can occur in-store, online, or through a combination of both.

Example 1: A retail clothing store sells its products directly to individual customers through its physical store locations. Customers visit the store, browse the merchandise, and make purchases for their personal use.

Example 2: An e-commerce website offers a wide range of consumer electronics, such as smartphones, laptops, and televisions. Consumers can browse the website, add products to their cart, and complete the purchase online for home delivery.

Example 3: A food delivery app allows consumers to order meals from various restaurants and have them delivered to their homes. Consumers can browse restaurant menus, place their orders, and make payments through the app.

Customer-Centric Approach: B2C businesses focus on meeting the needs and preferences of individual consumers. They tailor their products, services, and marketing strategies to appeal to a wide consumer base. B2C companies strive to provide a positive customer experience, convenience, and value to their target market.

Example 1: A cosmetics brand conducts market research to understand consumer preferences and trends. They use this information to develop and market new products that align with customer demands and expectations.

Example 2: An online grocery delivery service offers a user-friendly platform with personalised product recommendations and convenient delivery options to enhance the shopping experience for customers.

Example 3: An online streaming service analyses consumer viewing patterns and preferences to provide personalised content recommendations and curated playlists based on individual user interests.

Marketing and Sales Strategies: B2C companies employ various marketing and sales strategies to reach and engage with individual consumers. These strategies often involve targeted advertising, social media campaigns, influencer marketing, loyalty programs, and discounts or promotions.

Example 1: A global fast-food chain runs television and digital advertising campaigns to promote new menu items and limited-time offers, targeting consumers of all age groups.

Example 2: A beauty brand collaborates with social media influencers to showcase their products and share personal experiences, aiming to connect with and influence their followers' purchasing decisions.

Example 3: An online travel agency offers exclusive deals and discounts to customers who subscribe to their email newsletters or join their loyalty program, incentivising repeat business and customer loyalty.

In summary, B2C transactions involve businesses selling products or services directly to individual consumers. B2C companies prioritise understanding consumer needs, providing a positive customer experience, and implementing effective marketing and sales strategies to connect with and serve their target market.

C2C, or consumer-to-consumer, refers to transactions, interactions, and relationships between individual consumers. In C2C transactions, individuals engage in direct buying and selling of products or services with other individuals through various platforms and channels. C2C interactions often take place through online marketplaces, classified advertisements, peer-to-peer sharing platforms, and social media networks. Here is a detailed explanation of C2C along with three examples:

C2C Transactions: C2C transactions involve individuals buying and selling products or services directly to other individuals. These transactions can include the sale of used items, handmade crafts, personal services, or even renting out properties. Online platforms and marketplaces facilitate C2C transactions by connecting buyers and sellers.

Example 1: A person sells their used furniture through an online classified advertisement platform. Another individual interested in purchasing furniture finds the listing, contacts the seller, and completes the transaction.

Example 2: A photographer offers their services for hire on a freelance marketplace platform. Clients looking for a photographer browse the platform, view the photographer's portfolio, and directly contact them to discuss their requirements.

Example 3: An individual rents out their spare room through a peer-to-peer accommodation platform, where travellers can search for available listings, communicate with the host, and book a stay directly.

Individual Empowerment: C2C interactions empower individuals to become entrepreneurs or monetise their skills and assets. It allows people to leverage their resources and expertise to generate income, showcase their talents, and engage in economic activities on their terms.

Example 1: An artist creates handmade jewellery and sells it through an online marketplace, enabling them to reach a wider audience and establish a small business from their creative passion.

Example 2: A musician uploads their original songs on a music-sharing platform, allowing them to gain exposure, attract listeners, and potentially generate revenue through streaming or sales.

Example 3: A tutor offers online tutoring services in various subjects, connecting with students globally through an online tutoring platform and providing personalised academic support.

Online Platforms and Trust Mechanisms: C2C transactions heavily rely on online platforms that provide a marketplace for individuals to connect, communicate, and conduct transactions. These platforms often implement trust mechanisms, such as user ratings and reviews, to establish credibility and ensure safe interactions.

Example 1: An online marketplace for second-hand goods allows buyers and sellers to rate and review each other after completing a transaction. These ratings and reviews provide transparency and help build trust among users.

Example 2: A ride-sharing platform allows passengers to rate and review drivers based on their experience. This feedback system helps maintain quality and safety standards within the platform.

Example 3: A freelance services platform allows clients to leave feedback and ratings for freelancers they have hired. This helps establish the reputation and credibility of individual freelancers within the platform.

In summary, C2C transactions involve individuals directly buying and selling products or services with each other. C2C interactions enable individuals to engage in economic activities, monetise their skills, and leverage online platforms to connect and transact with a wider audience. Trust mechanisms implemented by these platforms help foster credibility and ensure safe transactions between individuals.

B: Products vs Services in Focus

A product company refers to an organisation that primarily focuses on the development, production, and sale of tangible or intangible products. These companies create and sell products that serve consumer needs, ranging from physical goods such as electronics and appliances to software applications and digital services. Here are five examples of product companies:

Apple Inc.: Apple is known for its range of consumer electronics, including the iPhone, Mac computers, iPad, and Apple Watch. They design, develop, and market innovative hardware and software products.

Procter & Gamble: P&G is a multinational consumer goods company that produces and sells a wide range of products such as cleaning agents, personal care items, and hygiene products. Their brand portfolio includes popular names like Pampers, Gillette, Tide, and Crest.

Microsoft Corporation: Microsoft is a technology company that develops and sells software, hardware, and cloud-based services. They offer products like the Windows operating system, Microsoft Office suite, Xbox gaming consoles, and Azure cloud platform.

Nike Inc.: Nike is a leading sports footwear and apparel company that designs, manufactures, and markets athletic shoes, apparel, and accessories. They are renowned for their brand presence and sponsorships in the sports industry.

Tesla Inc.: Tesla is an electric vehicle and clean energy company that designs, manufactures, and sells electric cars, solar energy products, and energy storage solutions. They are at the forefront of sustainable transportation and energy innovation.

Advantages of Working for Product Companies:

Product Innovation: Product companies often prioritise innovation and invest in research and development. Working for a product company gives employees the opportunity to be part of cutting-edge technologies, explore new ideas, and contribute to the development of innovative products.

Industry Recognition: Established product companies often have a strong brand presence and reputation in their respective industries. Being associated with a well-known and respected brand can enhance an employee's professional profile and provide recognition in the market.

Career Growth Opportunities: Product companies often offer structured career paths and growth opportunities. Employees can progress through various roles and responsibilities, gaining valuable experience and expanding their skill set within the organisation.

Collaboration and Teamwork: Developing and launching products requires collaborative efforts from cross-functional teams. Working for a product company allows employees to collaborate with professionals from different disciplines, fostering teamwork and building interpersonal skills.

Impact and Consumer Reach: Successful products from product companies can have a wide consumer reach and significant impact on people's lives. Being part of a company that creates products that resonate with consumers can provide a sense of fulfilment and pride.

Disadvantages of Working for Product Companies:

Market Competition: Product companies often operate in highly competitive markets, which can lead to intense pressure to innovate, meet customer demands, and stay ahead of competitors. This can result in high expectations and demanding work environments.

Market Volatility: Product companies may face challenges related to market fluctuations and changing consumer preferences. Economic downturns or shifts in trends can impact product demand and company stability, potentially leading to layoffs or downsizing.

Rigid Processes and Hierarchies: Established product companies may have established processes, structures, and hierarchies that can limit flexibility and agility. Decision-making and implementation of new ideas may require multiple levels of approvals and longer timeframes.

Product Development Risks: Developing and launching new products involve risks such as high development costs, uncertain market acceptance, and potential product failures. This can create uncertainty and job instability, particularly for employees directly involved in product development.

Limited Focus: Working for a product company often means focusing on a specific product or product line. This narrow focus may restrict exposure to other industries or areas of interest, limiting professional diversification and broader skill development.

It's important to note that the advantages and disadvantages can vary depending on the specific product company, industry, and individual preferences. It's advisable to thoroughly research and consider these factors before making career decisions.

A **service company** is an organisation that primarily offers intangible services or expertise to clients or customers. These companies focus on providing specialised services rather than tangible products. Here are five examples of service companies:

Deloitte: Deloitte is a multinational professional services firm that offers services in areas such as auditing, consulting, tax advisory, and financial advisory. They provide expertise and solutions to help clients navigate complex business challenges.

Airbnb: Airbnb is an online marketplace and hospitality service that enables individuals to list, discover, and book accommodations around the world. They connect hosts who offer lodging services with travellers seeking unique and personalised experiences.

Amazon Web Services (AWS): AWS is a subsidiary of Amazon that provides on-demand cloud computing platforms and services to individuals, companies, and governments. They offer a wide range of cloud-based services such as storage, databases, analytics, and artificial intelligence.

Uber: Uber is a ride-sharing and transportation network company that connects riders with drivers through a mobile app. They provide a convenient and on-demand transportation service to customers in various locations worldwide.

Accenture: Accenture is a global professional services company that offers services in consulting, technology, and outsourcing. They provide a wide range of solutions to help clients improve their business performance and achieve their strategic goals.

Advantages of Working for Service Companies:

Skill Development: Service companies often provide opportunities for employees to develop and enhance their skills in specific areas such as consulting, customer service, or technology. Working in these companies can help individuals build expertise and advance their careers in specialised domains.

Client Interaction: Service companies typically involve direct client interaction, allowing employees to develop strong interpersonal and communication skills. This exposure to clients can help individuals understand client needs, build relationships, and gain valuable client management experience.

Continuous Learning: Service companies often prioritise learning and professional development. They offer training programs, certifications, and access to industry-leading resources, allowing employees to continually update their knowledge and stay at the forefront of their field.

Variety of Projects: Service companies often work on a range of projects across different industries and clients. This variety offers employees the opportunity to work on diverse assignments, gain exposure to different business contexts, and develop a broader skill set.

Teamwork and Collaboration: Service companies emphasise teamwork and collaboration as projects often require coordinated efforts from multidisciplinary teams. This fosters a collaborative work environment, enabling employees to work alongside experts from different backgrounds and learn from their experiences.

Disadvantages of Working for Service Companies:

Workload and Deadlines: Service companies often operate in fast-paced environments, where tight deadlines and demanding client expectations are common. This can result in high workloads, long hours, and potential work-life balance challenges.

Client Demands and Pressures: Working in a service-oriented environment means that client satisfaction and meeting their expectations become top priorities. Employees may face high-pressure situations and the need to manage client demands effectively.

Project-based Uncertainty: Service companies often operate on a project-by-project basis, which can lead to periods of uncertainty between projects or assignments. Employees may need to adapt to changing project demands and potentially face gaps between assignments.

Service Quality Challenges: As service companies rely on delivering high-quality services, maintaining consistent service standards across various projects and clients can be challenging. Employees may need to manage expectations, handle service-related issues, and ensure client satisfaction.

Limited Tangible Output: Unlike product companies, service companies primarily offer intangible services, which can sometimes make it difficult to measure and showcase the direct impact of one's work. This can be a disadvantage for those seeking tangible, visible outcomes.

It's important to note that the advantages and disadvantages can vary depending on the specific service company, industry, and individual preferences. It's advisable to thoroughly research and consider these factors before making career decisions.

C: Business Model: Foundations

A business model is a framework or plan that outlines how a company creates, delivers, and captures value. It encompasses the key elements of a company's strategy, operations, and revenue generation. Here are some important business models commonly used by companies:

B2C (Business-to-Consumer): In the B2C model, companies sell products or services directly to individual consumers. This model is often associated with retail businesses, e-commerce platforms, and service providers targeting individual customers.

B2B (Business-to-Business): In the B2B model, companies sell products or services to other businesses. This model focuses on meeting the needs of business clients and often involves long-term contracts, customised solutions, and strategic partnerships.

Marketplace: The marketplace model involves creating a platform that connects buyers and sellers. The platform provider earns revenue through transaction fees, commissions, or subscriptions. Examples include e-commerce marketplaces, freelance platforms, and sharing economy platforms.

Subscription: The subscription model offers products or services to customers on a recurring basis in exchange for a subscription fee. This model provides predictable revenue streams and fosters customer loyalty. Examples include streaming services, software-as-a-service (SaaS), and membership-based businesses.

Freemium: The freemium model offers a basic version of a product or service for free, while charging for premium features or additional functionality. This model allows companies to attract a large user base and monetise through upgrades or added services. Examples include freemium software, mobile apps, and content platforms.

Franchise: The franchise model involves granting individuals or entities the right to operate under an established brand and business model in exchange for fees or royalties. Franchisees benefit from brand recognition and support from the franchisor. Examples include fast-food chains, hotel chains, and retail franchises.

Asset Light: The asset light model focuses on minimising the ownership of physical assets and instead leveraging partnerships, outsourcing, or sharing resources. This model reduces capital investment and allows companies to focus on core competencies. Examples include ride-sharing platforms and hospitality platforms.

Razor and Blade: The razor and blade model involves selling a primary product or device at a low cost or even at a loss, while making profits from the sales of complementary or consumable products. Examples include printers and ink cartridges, gaming consoles and game titles, and coffee machines and coffee pods.

Direct-to-Consumer (D2C): The D2C model involves companies selling their products or services directly to customers without intermediaries. This allows for greater control over the customer experience, data, and branding. Examples include D2C fashion brands, personal care brands, and home goods brands.

Platform-as-a-Service (PaaS): The PaaS model provides a platform that allows developers to build, deploy, and manage applications. Companies charge for usage of the platform and related services, providing developers with the infrastructure they need without the need for extensive hardware investments. Examples include cloud computing platforms like AWS and Microsoft Azure.

These are just a few examples of important business models. Each model has its unique characteristics, revenue streams, and value propositions. Companies often adapt and combine multiple models to suit their specific industry, target market, and competitive landscape.

D: Beyond Profits: The World of Non-Business Models

Non-business models refer to frameworks or structures adopted by organisations or entities that are not primarily driven by profit-making motives. These models are often associated with nonprofit organisations, government agencies, community initiatives, and social enterprises. Here are some examples of non-business models:

Nonprofit Organisation: Nonprofit organisations operate for a social or charitable purpose rather than generating profits. They rely on funding from donations, grants, and sponsorships to support their activities. Examples include charitable foundations, educational institutions, healthcare organisations, and environmental conservation groups.

Government Agency: Government agencies are entities established and funded by the government to provide public services and regulate specific sectors. These agencies are responsible for implementing policies, enforcing regulations, and delivering public programs. Examples include tax authorities, public health agencies, transportation departments, and regulatory bodies.

Cooperative: Cooperatives are organisations owned and operated by their members, who share resources and collectively make decisions. They aim to meet the needs of their members and the community rather than maximising profits. Examples include agricultural cooperatives, credit unions, and worker cooperatives.

Social Enterprise: Social enterprises are organisations that use business methods and strategies to address social or environmental challenges. They aim to generate revenue while also creating a positive impact on society. Examples include fair trade organisations, social impact ventures, and community development projects.

Community-based Initiative: Community-based initiatives involve collective efforts within a specific community or locality to address local needs and enhance the well-being of community members. These initiatives often rely on volunteer work, community participation, and local resources. Examples include community gardens, neighborhood associations, and grassroots organizations.

Academic Institution: Academic institutions, such as universities and research centres, operate under a non-business model focused on education, research, and knowledge dissemination. Their primary objective is to provide quality education and contribute to intellectual development and advancement in various fields.

Cultural and Arts Organizations: Cultural and arts organizations, such as museums, galleries, theatres, and cultural centres, operate to preserve and promote artistic, historical, and cultural heritage. They often rely on funding from grants, sponsorships, and ticket sales to sustain their operations and provide cultural experiences to the public.

Foundations: Foundations are organizations established with a specific mission or cause and provide funding and support to other organizations or initiatives aligned with their goals. They often distribute grants, scholarships, or resources to advance research, education, social causes, or community development.

Faith-based Organizations: Faith-based organizations operate based on religious principles and serve the spiritual, social, and charitable needs of their members and the wider community. They engage in activities such as religious services, community outreach, humanitarian aid, and advocacy.

Advocacy Groups: Advocacy groups work towards promoting specific causes, influencing public opinion, and advocating for policy changes. They raise awareness, mobilise support, and engage in activities like lobbying, public campaigns, and community education.

These non-business models prioritise social impact, community service, public benefit, and the advancement of specific causes rather than profit generation. They rely on different funding sources, such as donations, grants, government funding, and collaborations, to support their operations and achieve their mission.

Conclusion

"Decoding Business Types" provides clarity on diverse business models – B2B (Business to Business), B2C (Business to Consumer), and C2C (Consumer to Consumer). This section underscores the importance of understanding these models to tailor strategies effectively for target markets and audiences.

"Products vs Services in Focus" explores the distinctions between product and service-oriented businesses. This section emphasises the unique challenges and strategies associated with each, guiding businesses to align their approaches with the nature of their offerings for your job.

"Business Model: Foundations" delves into the core components that form the basis of a successful business model. This section encourages businesses to critically evaluate and refine their models, considering key elements such as value proposition, revenue streams, and cost structures.

"Beyond Profits: The World of Non-Business Models" explores models that extend beyond traditional profit-centric approaches. This section introduces the concept of non-business models, emphasising social enterprises, nonprofits, and other models driven by purposes beyond financial gain. The key takeaway is the recognition that diverse models exist, each with its unique goals and impacts.

In summary, "Exploring Business Landscapes" provides a comprehensive overview of the varied terrain within the business world. It guides readers in understanding different business types, the nuances of products and services, the foundational elements of business models, and the emergence of non-business models that prioritise social and environmental impact alongside financial success. This knowledge equips individuals and businesses to navigate the diverse landscapes, make informed decisions, and align their strategies with their specific goals and values.

E: Effective Questions to Ask the Leaders

- How does our company differentiate its approach when dealing with B2B, B2C, and C2C interactions?
- What are the key challenges and opportunities associated with each of these business models?
- Can you provide examples of successful B2B partnerships that our company has formed?
- How do we tailor our marketing and communication strategies for B2C customers to ensure effective engagement and conversion?
- What strategies do we employ to build trust and facilitate successful C2C transactions on our platform?
- How does our company's approach differ when offering products versus services to our customers?
- What are the main advantages and disadvantages of focusing on our product-based offerings?
- Can you provide examples of successful product launches or innovations within our company?
- How do we ensure high-quality service delivery and customer satisfaction in our service-based offerings?
- What strategies do we use to differentiate our products or services from competitors in the market?
- Can you explain the core elements of our company's business model and how they contribute to our overall success?
- What are the key revenue streams and value propositions of our business model?
- How do we continuously evaluate and adapt our business model to stay relevant in the market?
- Can you share examples of how our business model has evolved or been disrupted over time?
- What strategies do we employ to manage risks and uncertainties associated with our business model?
- How does our organisation's non-business model align with our mission and social impact goals?

- Can you provide examples of successful initiatives or projects that have been driven by our non-business model?
- What are the main funding sources or revenue streams that support our non-business activities?
- How do we measure the success and impact of our non-business initiatives?
- What strategies do we use to ensure sustainability and long-term growth within our non-business model framework?

Chapter VI

Crafting Your Work Paradigm

Why this Chapter?

Understanding work modes is like figuring out how different job roles work within a company. Just like how some students are good at maths while others are better at drawing or language, each person has their own style when it comes to working. I used to wonder why some people could write or draw so easily. Later, I realised that everyone has their strengths, and they also have a basic way they like to work on specific tasks.

Knowing about these work modes can help you decide which roles are a good fit for you and what kind of company or industry suits your way of working. Sometimes people mix different styles that work best for them on certain tasks. Learning to adjust your methods as needed is useful, but knowing the main work modes can give you a starting point to develop your own style.

Think of work modes as different styles or approaches to getting things done. Discovering these modes is like finding your own special way of doing things at work. This can guide you toward jobs that match your strengths and make your career journey smoother. It's also like finding the right puzzle piece for your professional identity, making your path clearer.

Even though some people mix work modes, having a good grasp of the main ones is helpful. It's like having a map that shows you where to start when you're developing your own way of working. In the big picture of careers, understanding work modes is like knowing yourself better. It helps you create a career that fits you well, where you can be creative and successful in your own unique way.

A: Navigating a Process-Oriented Framework

Imagine the process-oriented work mode as a step-by-step recipe for success. It's all about following a set plan to get things done smoothly and correctly.

Here's how it goes:

Stick to the Plan: Just like when you follow a recipe to bake cookies, in this mode, you're sticking to a plan or a series of steps.

Efficiency Matters: Imagine you're trying to build a LEGO set as quickly as possible. That's what you do in the process-oriented mode – you're all about getting things done efficiently.

No Surprises: Just like when you know what ingredients to use in a recipe, in this mode, you're not trying out new things. You're following a tried-and-tested way of doing things.

Getting Consistent Results: Think of it like making a perfect pancake every time because you use the same measurements. In the process-oriented mode, you're all about getting consistent and reliable results.

Improving How You Work: Just like tweaking a recipe to make it even tastier, in this mode, you're always looking for ways to make your work process better and more effective.

It's like being a methodical chef in the kitchen. You're not winging it – you're following a plan that helps you get things done accurately and efficiently.

Here are a Few Examples of How the Process-Oriented Work Mode is Applied in Different Industries:

Manufacturing Industry: In manufacturing plants, the process-oriented work mode is crucial for ensuring efficient production lines. Workers follow standardised processes to assemble products, ensuring consistency and quality. This work mode helps minimise errors and allows for smooth coordination among different stages of production.

Call Centres: Call centres heavily rely on the process-oriented work mode to provide consistent customer support experiences. Customer service representatives follow scripted protocols when assisting customers, ensuring that all relevant information is collected and communicated effectively. This work mode helps maintain a high level of service quality and ensures that customer inquiries are handled efficiently.

Software Development: In the field of software development, the process-oriented work mode is often implemented through agile methodologies such as Scrum or Kanban. These methodologies provide structured processes and frameworks for managing project development, including defining requirements, breaking down tasks into manageable units, and establishing iterative and incremental development cycles. This work mode allows development teams to maintain transparency, collaborate effectively, and deliver high-quality software within set timelines.

Overall, the process-oriented work mode focuses on establishing efficient workflows, standardising procedures, and ensuring consistency in task execution. It enables organisations to optimise their operations, improve productivity, and maintain high levels of quality in their products or services.

B: Cultivating Creative Brilliance in Your Work

Imagine the creative work mode as a playground for your mind. It's all about letting your imagination run wild, coming up with cool ideas, and trying out new things.

Here's How It Works:

Thinking Outside the Box: In this mode, you're not sticking to the usual stuff. You're thinking in new and different ways. It's like colouring outside the lines.

Innovative Ideas: Imagine you're inventing a new game. That's what you do in the creative mode – come up with fresh and unique ideas that no one thought of before.

Taking Risks: Just like trying out a new trick on the playground, in creative mode, you're not afraid to take risks. You're willing to try things that might be a little different.

Pushing Boundaries: Creative mode is like exploring uncharted territory. You're not afraid to go beyond the limits and break the rules a bit.

Finding Unique Solutions: Imagine you're building a cool new toy using random stuff you find. In creative mode, you find creative solutions that are totally unique.

It's like being an artist, inventor, and explorer all at once. You're not following the usual path – you're making your own way with your creative thinking.

Here are a Few Examples of How the Creative Work Mode is Applied in Different Industries:

Advertising and Marketing: In the advertising industry, creative work mode is essential for developing attention-grabbing campaigns. Creative teams brainstorm unique concepts, design compelling visuals, and craft persuasive messages to engage and captivate target audiences. This work mode encourages thinking beyond traditional advertising techniques and finding inventive ways to communicate messages effectively.

Design and Fashion: The creative work mode is inherent in the design and fashion industries. Designers embrace creativity to develop original and visually appealing products, whether it's clothing, furniture, or graphic designs. They draw inspiration from various sources, experiment with different materials, and push the boundaries of conventional design to create innovative and aesthetically pleasing outcomes.

Product Development: Creative work mode is crucial in the field of product development, where companies strive to create groundbreaking and unique products. Teams engage in brainstorming sessions, prototype development, and iterative design processes to come up with innovative features, functionalities, and user experiences. This work mode encourages experimentation, risk-taking, and exploring novel ideas to create products that stand out in the market.

Overall, the creative work mode encourages individuals to think beyond conventional approaches, embrace innovation, and explore new possibilities. It fosters an environment that values imagination, originality, and the freedom to take risks, leading to the development of fresh ideas and groundbreaking solutions.

C: Knowledge Sharing: Harnessing Peer-to-Peer Learning

Peer-to-peer learning is like a group study session at work. It's about teaming up with your colleagues to share what you know and learn from each other.

Here's How It Goes:

Sharing What You Know: Imagine you're good at something, like solving maths problems. In this mode, you'd share your maths-solving skills with your colleagues. They might know things you don't, and you might have some tricks they haven't heard of.

Learning from Others: Just like you teach maths to your friends, they might teach you something else. You learn from their experiences, insights, and skills.

Supportive Environment: It's like a friendly club where everyone helps each other. You create an atmosphere where everyone feels comfortable sharing their knowledge.

Learning Together: In this mode, everyone grows together. You work on projects, discuss ideas, and learn from each other's successes and mistakes.

Different Ways to Learn: Peer-to-peer learning isn't just one thing. It can be a mentor showing you the ropes, a coworker teaching you a new tool, or a team collaborating on a project.

Think of it as studying for a test, but instead of textbooks, you're using your colleagues' expertise. It's a team effort where everyone helps each other shine.

Here are a Few Examples of How Peer-to-Peer Learning is Applied in Different Contexts:

Mentorship Programmes: Many organisations establish formal mentorship programmes where experienced employees mentor and guide junior or less experienced colleagues. Through regular interactions, the mentors share their knowledge, provide guidance, and offer support to help mentees enhance their skills, grow professionally, and navigate their career paths.

Cross-Functional Collaboration: Peer-to-peer learning is facilitated when employees from different departments or teams collaborate on projects or initiatives. By working together, individuals with diverse expertise and perspectives can learn from each other, exchange best practices, and gain a broader understanding of the organisation's operations.

Knowledge Sharing Sessions: Organisations can host knowledge-sharing sessions, workshops, or brown bag lunches where employees have the opportunity to present on specific topics, share their expertise, and engage in discussions. These sessions encourage individuals to learn from their peers, ask questions, and gather insights from different perspectives.

Peer-to-peer learning fosters a culture of continuous learning and professional development within an organisation. It promotes collaboration, strengthens relationships among employees, and harnesses the collective knowledge and expertise of the workforce. By tapping into the experiences and insights of colleagues, individuals can broaden their skill sets, gain new perspectives, and enhance their overall performance.

It's important to create an environment that encourages and supports peer-to-peer learning by providing resources, recognition, and opportunities for collaboration. When employees actively participate in sharing their knowledge and learning from others, it creates a culture of continuous improvement and development throughout the organisation.

D: Crack Analytical Work

Imagine the analytical work mode as being a detective for tasks and projects. It's all about using your thinking cap, crunching data, and making decisions based on facts.

Here's How It Works:

Thinking Critically: In this mode, you're like a puzzle solver. You break big problems into smaller pieces and look at them one by one. It's like investigating a crime scene, step by step.

Gathering Clues: Just like a detective collects clues, you gather data and info. You use tools and methods to get the facts you need.

Spotting Patterns: Detectives notice patterns in clues, right? Similarly, in analytical mode, you spot patterns and trends in the data you've collected.

Drawing Conclusions: Detectives piece together evidence to solve a case. In analytical mode, you use the info you've gathered to make decisions that make sense.

Being Systematic: Just like detectives have a plan, you've got a method. You follow a step-by-step process to make sure you're not missing anything important.

Think of it as being the Sherlock Holmes of work. You're the one who digs deep, looks for evidence, and connects the dots to solve the mysteries of tasks and projects.

Here are a Few Examples of How the Analytical Work Mode is Applied in Different Contexts:

Data Analysis: Analytical work mode often involves working with large datasets to extract meaningful insights. This can include analysing customer data, market trends, financial reports, or operational metrics. Through techniques such as statistical analysis, data mining, and visualisation, individuals can identify patterns, correlations, and trends that inform decision-making.

Problem Solving: Analytical work mode is crucial in problem-solving scenarios. It involves breaking down complex problems into smaller, solvable parts and then systematically applying analytical frameworks to examine each part. By evaluating the available information, identifying potential causes, and analysing the implications of different solutions, individuals can make well-informed decisions to address the problem effectively.

Forecasting and Planning: In an analytical work mode, individuals use historical data, market trends, and other relevant factors to forecast future outcomes and plan accordingly. This can involve conducting market research, financial modelling, scenario analysis, or risk assessment. By analysing data and using forecasting techniques, individuals can make informed predictions and develop strategic plans to guide business decisions.

Analytical work mode requires individuals to have strong analytical and problem-solving skills, attention to detail, and a logical mindset. It also involves the ability to work with data, use analytical tools and software, and effectively communicate findings and recommendations to stakeholders.

By employing an analytical work mode, organisations can make data-driven decisions, identify opportunities for improvement, and mitigate risks. It helps foster a culture of evidence-based decision-making, continuous improvement, and strategic thinking within the organisation.

E: Agility in Action: Embracing an Agile Workstyle

Agile work mode is like being a flexible and responsive team player. It started in software development but has spread to other areas too.

Here's How It Works:

Taking Small Steps: Instead of tackling a big project all at once, you break it into smaller parts, called iterations. You work on these chunks one at a time, delivering value in stages. This means you can get feedback along the way and make changes as needed.

Teamwork All the Way: In agile mode, it's all about teamwork. People with different skills team up to work on a project. This mix of talents brings fresh ideas and viewpoints. Everyone works closely, making decisions together and sharing responsibility.

Change is OK: Agile knows that change happens. It's ready to adapt to new requirements or shifts in the market. Teams can quickly adjust their plans to stay on track and keep delivering what's most important.

Let the Data Guide You: Decisions aren't just based on gut feelings. Agile relies on data and feedback from customers, users, and stakeholders. This helps teams make smart choices and test their assumptions.

Keep Learning and Growing: Agile never stops learning. After each iteration, teams look back to see what went well and what could be better. They try out new ideas and learn from past experiences to keep improving.

Think of it as a way of working that's not rigid but open to change and growth. It's like a toolbox that helps teams build better, adapt faster, and learn continuously.

Examples of Agile Work Mode in Action:

Software Development: Agile methodologies such as Scrum and Kanban are commonly used in software development. Teams work in short iterations, collaborate closely, and regularly demonstrate working software to stakeholders. They adapt their plans based on feedback and prioritise the most valuable features.

Marketing Campaigns: Agile work mode can be applied to marketing campaigns where teams work in short cycles to plan, execute, and evaluate campaigns. They gather data and feedback to optimise campaign performance, adjust messaging based on market trends, and continuously refine their strategies.

Product Development: Agile work mode is often employed in product development processes. Cross-functional teams work together to develop minimum viable products (MVPs) and gather feedback from users. They use this feedback to iterate and refine the product, ensuring it meets customer needs and aligns with market demands.

By adopting Agile work mode, organisations can improve their ability to respond to changing market conditions, deliver value to customers more efficiently, and foster a culture of continuous improvement and collaboration. It enables teams to embrace change, adapt quickly, and deliver high-quality outcomes in a dynamic and fast-paced environment.

F: Customer-Centric Excellence: Focusing on What Matters

Customer-focused work mode is like putting customers at the heart of everything you do. It means really getting into the minds of your customers and making sure you're giving them exactly what they need and want.

In this approach, you shift your mindset to be all about the customer. You're not just ticking off tasks; you're putting in the effort to make sure customers have an amazing experience.

So, how does this work? You start by getting to know your customers really well. What do they like? What do they struggle with? What are they hoping to achieve? When you have these insights, you can tailor what you're offering—whether it's products, services, or even just a friendly chat—to match exactly what they're looking for.

It's like being a super attentive host at a party, making sure every guest has a great time. When you're in customer-focused mode, you're creating experiences that leave customers feeling happy and satisfied. And that's not just good for them; it's good for your business too.

Here are a Few Examples of How Customer-Focused Work Mode is Applied in Different Contexts:

Market Research: Customer-focused work mode often involves conducting market research to gather insights about customer preferences, behaviours, and trends. This can include surveys, interviews, focus groups, and data analysis to understand customer needs and expectations. The findings from market research inform decision-making and help shape product development, marketing strategies, and customer service initiatives.

Customer Experience Design: In a customer-focused work mode, individuals work on designing and improving the end-to-end customer experience. This includes mapping out customer journeys, identifying pain points, and finding opportunities to enhance customer satisfaction. By understanding the touchpoints where customers interact with the organisation, individuals can optimise these interactions to create seamless, personalised, and delightful experiences.

Customer Service and Support: Customer-focused work mode extends to customer service and support functions. Individuals in these roles prioritise responsiveness, empathy, and problem-solving to address customer inquiries, concerns, and issues. They strive to provide exceptional service and go above and beyond to exceed customer expectations.

Customer-focused work mode requires individuals to actively listen to customers, empathise with their needs, and continuously seek ways to enhance their experiences. It involves strong communication and interpersonal skills, as well as a commitment to building long-term relationships with customers.

By adopting a customer-focused work mode, organisations can build customer loyalty, drive customer satisfaction, and gain a competitive advantage in the market. It helps create a customer-centric culture where all employees are aligned towards delivering exceptional value and exceeding customer expectations at every touchpoint.

G: The Art of Being Easy to Work With

No matter where you stand in your career journey or how you approach your work, being easy to work with is a game-changer that often gets overlooked. You see, those who are difficult to work with often carry around an ego that's hard to miss. This ego might stem from their impressive degrees, prestigious education, job titles, hefty paychecks, vast knowledge, or extensive experience. It's like they're wearing a badge that says "Look at me and my greatness."

But here's the truth about the long run: those ego-driven folks don't leave a lasting mark. And down the road, if you're thinking of starting your own business or need support from high-level contacts, that network you've built won't be there to lend a hand, even if they could.

So, you might be wondering, how do you become that person who's easy to work with? Well, guess what? It's not as complicated as it might seem.

Step one: Make sure you're an asset to the team. We all stumble and fall at some point, but showing strong effort and dedication to a task can make up for any missteps. It's like turning failure into a learning opportunity.

Step two: Be both a seeker and a giver of help. Nobody's perfect, and we all need a little support in areas where we're not experts. If there's something you're struggling with, don't hesitate to ask for help. And if someone else needs a hand, be there to offer yours.

Step three: Embrace feedback like a champ. Not all feedback is off the mark, even if your intentions were spot-on. Sometimes, your hard work and good intentions might be seen differently by others. It's like projecting a message that gets misinterpreted. So, be open to adjusting how you communicate your intentions.

Step four: Be the reliable one. Everyone loves working with someone they can count on. You might not be best of buddies with all your colleagues, and that's okay. But if you're the person who consistently delivers assigned tasks on time, you'll earn admiration and appreciation.

Remember, in the grand scheme of things, being easy to work with leaves a much more positive mark than flaunting your ego. So, as you navigate your career, keep these steps in mind. They're like keys to opening doors of opportunity, respect, and collaboration in the world of work.

In summary, for a work mode framework, depending on the job role and responsibilities, individuals may need to blend multiple work modes to excel in their work. For example, a project manager may need to adopt a process-oriented work mode to ensure project milestones are met, a creative work mode to devise innovative project strategies, a peer-to-peer learning work mode to collaborate with team members, and an analytical work mode to analyze project data and make informed decisions.

By recognizing the different work modes and developing the ability to switch between them as required, individuals can enhance their effectiveness, contribute to the organization's success, and excel in their respective roles. It is important to be adaptable, open-minded, and continuously develop the skills needed for each work mode to thrive in today's diverse and dynamic work environments.

Conclusion

"Navigating a Process-Oriented Framework" introduces the importance of structured processes in achieving work efficiency. This section encourages individuals to understand and optimize workflows, fostering a systematic approach for enhanced productivity.

"Cultivating Creative Brilliance in Your Work" emphasizes the role of creativity in problem-solving and innovation. This section advocates for cultivating a creative mindset, embracing diverse perspectives, and incorporating imaginative thinking into everyday tasks.

"Knowledge Sharing: Harnessing Peer-to-Peer Learning" highlights the power of collaborative learning within a team. This section encourages individuals to actively share insights, skills, and experiences, fostering a culture of continuous learning and growth.

"Crack Analytical Work" delves into the art of analytical thinking. This section emphasizes the importance of critical analysis, data interpretation, and problem-solving skills in making informed decisions and driving successful outcomes.

"Agility in Action: Embracing an Agile Workstyle" champions adaptability and flexibility in the workplace. This section encourages individuals and teams to embrace an agile mindset, allowing for quick responses to change, innovation, and evolving project requirements.

"Customer-Centric Excellence: Focusing on What Matters" centers on the significance of prioritizing customer needs. This section advocates for a customer-centric approach, emphasizing the importance of understanding, anticipating, and exceeding customer expectations for business success.

"The Art of Being Easy to Work With" underscores the importance of interpersonal skills and collaboration. This section encourages individuals to cultivate a positive work demeanor, effective communication, and a collaborative attitude, contributing to a harmonious and productive work environment.

In essence, "Crafting Your Work Paradigm" is a holistic guide that encourages individuals to navigate their professional journey with a balanced blend of process orientation, creativity, collaborative learning, analytical thinking, agility, customer focus, and effective interpersonal skills. By embracing these principles, individuals can shape a work paradigm that is not only efficient and productive but also conducive to personal and collective growth.

H: Effective Questions to Ask the Leaders

- How would you define our organization's work modes, and how do they influence the way we approach our work?
- Which work mode(s) do you think are most important for our team or department? Why?
- Can you provide examples of projects or situations where adopting a specific work mode was particularly effective?
- How can I identify the most suitable work mode for a specific task or project?
- Are there any specific skills or competencies that are valuable for each work mode? How can I develop those skills?
- How can I leverage different work modes to enhance my performance and contribute more effectively to team projects?
- Are there any training or development opportunities available to improve my understanding and application of different work modes?
- Can you share any strategies or tips for balancing and transitioning between different work modes effectively?

- How can I align my personal work style and preferences with the organization's preferred work modes?
- Are there any tools or technologies that can support and enhance the implementation of different work modes?
- Can you provide feedback or guidance on how I can better incorporate collaborative and team-oriented work modes into my projects?
- What role does creativity play in our work modes, and how can I foster and encourage creativity in my own work?
- How can I incorporate agile work modes into my project management approach to increase flexibility and adaptability?
- Are there any specific metrics or indicators we use to evaluate the effectiveness of different work modes in achieving project goals?
- Can you provide examples of how customer-focused work modes have influenced our products or services and led to success?
- How can I contribute to a culture of peer-to-peer learning within our team or department?
- What strategies can I employ to develop a more analytical mindset and approach to problem-solving in my work?
- Are there any industry trends or developments that are influencing the adoption of different work modes within our organization?
- Can you share any success stories or case studies where implementing a specific work mode led to significant positive outcomes?
- How can I collaborate with colleagues from different departments or teams to leverage their expertise and adopt a more process-oriented work mode?

Chapter VII

Steering Relationship

Why this Chapter?

Managing relationships is like taking care of a special garden filled with people you know. If you're in your 20s, you've probably seen lots of different relationships in your life, like family, friends, and romantic partners. Just like these relationships teach you things about yourself, work relationships can do the same if you look at them in a positive way.

We usually think of family and friends as important because we can easily see how they affect our lives. But we don't always realize that work relationships also have important lessons and tricks that can help us in our personal lives. What we really want is for others to understand us better.

Our brains aren't good at seeing the long-term benefits of relationships. We can't predict how people will change over time. Strangely, relationships are a bit like saving money for investment. The more you invest in them, the more they grow over time, even if you don't notice it right away. The people you get to know when you're young can become your partners in business when you're older, or even people who help you in your own business someday. They might even become your romantic partners. There are endless possibilities.

The cool thing is that the lessons you learn from your personal relationships can also help you in your work relationships, and the other way around. Learning how to listen, compromise, and trust are skills that work in all kinds of relationships. These skills, as you practice them, become useful tools in building relationships that can lead to exciting opportunities and long-lasting connections.

Here are Some Important Lessons to Consider for Effective Relationship Management:

Communication is Key: Clear and open communication is essential for building and maintaining strong relationships. It's important to actively listen, express yourself clearly, and be responsive. Regular and honest communication helps to establish trust and understanding.

Understand the Needs of Others: Take the time to understand the needs, expectations, and goals of the people you are interacting with. By understanding their perspectives, you can tailor your approach and actions to better meet their needs. This demonstrates empathy and shows that you value the relationship.

Build Trust and Credibility: Trust is the foundation of any successful relationship. Be reliable, consistent, and deliver on your commitments. Act with integrity and honesty and avoid making promises you cannot keep. Building trust takes time and effort, but it is crucial for long-term relationship management.

Foster Collaboration and Cooperation: Collaboration and cooperation are vital for successful relationships. Be willing to work together, share ideas, and find common ground. Encourage open dialogue, value diverse perspectives, and seek win-win solutions. By fostering a collaborative environment, you can build stronger and more mutually beneficial relationships.

Manage Conflict Constructively: Conflict is a natural part of any relationship, and it's important to address it constructively. Instead of avoiding or suppressing conflict, approach it with a problem-solving mindset. Seek to understand different viewpoints, find common ground, and work towards mutually acceptable resolutions. Effective conflict management can strengthen relationships and lead to better outcomes.

Be Empathetic and Respectful: Treat others with respect and empathy. Put yourself in their shoes and try to understand their emotions and perspectives. Show appreciation for their contributions and value their opinions. Being empathetic and respectful creates a positive atmosphere and fosters trust and mutual understanding.

Maintain Consistency and Long-Term Focus: Building and maintaining relationships is a long-term endeavour. Consistency in your actions, communication, and follow-through is essential. Strive to build enduring relationships rather than focusing solely on short-term gains. Investing in long-term relationships can lead to mutual growth and opportunities.

Adapt to Changing Dynamics: Relationships evolve over time, and it's important to adapt to changing dynamics. Be flexible, open to feedback, and willing to adjust your approach as needed. Embrace change and be proactive in nurturing and strengthening your relationships.

Show Appreciation and Recognition: Regularly express appreciation and recognise the contributions of others. Acknowledge their achievements, efforts, and impact on the relationship. Simple acts of gratitude can go a long way in building and maintaining strong relationships.

Continuously Invest in Relationships: Building and maintaining relationships require ongoing effort and investment. Regularly check in with others, maintain contact, and nurture connections. Seek opportunities to collaborate, support, and add value to the relationships. Consistent investment will help cultivate meaningful and mutually beneficial connections.

By incorporating these lessons into your relationship management approach, you can foster stronger, more productive, and harmonious relationships in both personal and professional settings.

A: Science of Building Rapport

Rapport building refers to the process of developing a positive and harmonious relationship with others, particularly with senior management and peers. It involves establishing a sense of trust, understanding, and mutual respect, contributing to effective communication, collaboration, and a productive work environment. Building rapport is essential in professional settings as it helps create a supportive and cohesive team, foster cooperation, and enhance overall job satisfaction.

When it comes to interacting with senior management and peers, rapport building plays a crucial role in establishing credibility, gaining influence, and forming valuable connections. It's about forming a positive bond that helps everyone work together smoothly and happily.

Here's How to Build Rapport:

Listen Up: Imagine you're having a chat with a friend, and you're really into what they're saying. That's active listening – paying full attention and showing that you care about what others have to say.

Just Be You: Think about how you act with your closest buddies – you're yourself, right? Same goes for building rapport. Be genuine and approachable, and people will trust and like you.

Respect is Key: Treat everyone with respect and keep things professional. When you show that you value others' knowledge and ideas, it makes a great impression.

Find What Connects You: Just like finding out that you and a friend both love the same TV show, look for common interests or goals with your colleagues. Sharing something in common brings people closer.

Talk Their Talk: Imagine you're chatting with a grandparent – you'd probably talk differently than with your buddies. Same goes here – adapt your communication style to match what others prefer.

Team Player: Offer to help out and work together with your colleagues and bosses. Sharing ideas and joining forces on projects creates a sense of unity.

Emotional IQ: Think about how you can tell when someone's happy or sad by their face. That's emotional intelligence – understanding emotions, including your own. It helps you relate better to others.

Keep Growing: Imagine you're getting better at your favourite video game with every level. In the same way, keep learning and improving your skills. It shows you're committed to being your best.

Walk the Talk: Remember how you trust a friend who always keeps their promises? Same goes in work. Be reliable and true to your word – it builds trust.

Remember that building rapport is an ongoing process that requires effort and attention. It takes time to establish strong relationships, and maintaining rapport requires consistent nurturing and investment. By focusing on effective communication, mutual respect, and shared goals, you can build rapport with senior management and peers, fostering a positive and collaborative work environment.

B: Networking Brilliance: Forging Lasting Connections

Networking plays a crucial role in professional growth and relationship building. It involves actively connecting and building relationships with individuals both within and outside your organisation. Let's explore networking in more detail:

Internal Organisational Network

Internal networking refers to building relationships within your own organisation. It involves connecting with colleagues, peers, supervisors, and employees from different departments. Here are two examples of internal networking:

Cross-Department Collaboration: Engage with individuals from different departments by actively participating in cross-functional projects or task forces. This allows you to expand your network within the organisation, gain exposure to different perspectives, and develop a broader understanding of the company's operations.

Informal Social Gatherings: Take advantage of informal social events such as team lunches, office parties, or after-work activities to connect with colleagues from various levels and departments. These relaxed settings provide an opportunity to build rapport, share experiences, and foster relationships beyond the confines of work-related discussions.

External Network

External networking involves building connections outside of your organisation. It enables you to expand your professional network, gain industry insights, and explore career opportunities beyond your current workplace. Here are two examples of external networking:

Professional Associations and Industry Events: Join professional associations or attend industry conferences, seminars, or workshops related to your field. These events provide an opportunity to meet professionals from various organisations, exchange knowledge, discuss industry trends, and establish connections that can benefit your career growth.

Online Networking Platforms: Utilise online platforms such as LinkedIn to connect with professionals in your industry. Actively engage in industry-specific groups or forums, share insights, participate in discussions, and reach out to individuals who share similar interests or expertise. These platforms offer a virtual space to expand your network, seek advice, and stay updated with industry news.

It is important to note that networking should be approached with sincerity, mutual benefit, and long-term relationship building in mind. It involves active listening, genuine interest in others, and a willingness to provide support or assistance when needed. Remember to maintain professionalism, follow up with connections, and offer value in your interactions to establish meaningful and lasting professional relationships.

C: Power of Reciprocity: Leveraging Favors Wisely

Leveraging your network and relationships in the context of work or job is crucial for career growth and professional success. Here are some important points on how to effectively leverage your network and relationships:

Build Genuine Relationships: Focus on building authentic and meaningful relationships with colleagues, supervisors, mentors, and industry professionals. Take the time to understand their interests, goals, and challenges. Show genuine care and support for their success.

Be a Resource and Add Value: Offer your skills, knowledge, and expertise to others in your network. Be proactive in helping them solve problems or achieve their goals. Providing value and being a resource to others strengthens your relationships and encourages reciprocity.

Maintain Regular Communication: Stay in touch with your network through regular communication channels, such as emails, phone calls, or in-person meetings. Keep them updated on your professional progress and accomplishments and show interest in their own endeavors.

Seek Advisors: Identify individuals who have achieved success in your desired field or industry and seek their guidance. Establishing mentor-mentee relationships can provide valuable insights, advice, and support throughout your career journey.

Attend Networking Events: Actively participate in professional networking events, industry conferences, and seminars. These gatherings provide opportunities to meet new people, exchange ideas, and expand your network. Be prepared with your elevator pitch and engage in meaningful conversations.

Utilise Online Networking Platforms: Leverage online platforms like LinkedIn to connect with professionals in your field. Engage in discussions, join relevant groups, and share valuable insights to establish your expertise and expand your online presence.

Give and Receive Recommendations: Offer recommendations to deserving colleagues and professionals within your network. Likewise, seek recommendations from trusted connections who can vouch for your skills and abilities. Positive recommendations can enhance your professional reputation.

Engage in Cross-Functional Projects: Seek out opportunities to collaborate with individuals from different departments or teams within your organisation. This helps broaden your network and allows you to gain exposure to different perspectives and expertise.

Stay Updated on Industry Trends: Keep yourself informed about industry trends, innovations, and developments. This knowledge positions you as a valuable resource and enables you to contribute meaningful insights during discussions and interactions.

Follow Up and Express Gratitude: After connecting with someone or receiving support, always follow up with a thank-you message or email. Expressing gratitude shows your appreciation and reinforces the positive impression you've made.

Remember, effective networking and relationship-building require consistent effort and nurturing. It's important to be genuine, authentic, and approachable in your interactions. By leveraging your network and relationships strategically, you can open doors to new opportunities, gain valuable insights, and advance your career.

Conclusion

"Science of Building Rapport" delves into the art and psychology of creating meaningful connections. This section emphasises the importance of authenticity, active listening, and shared understanding in establishing strong and genuine rapport with colleagues, clients, and partners.

"Networking Brilliance: Forging Lasting Connections" explores the strategic aspects of networking. This section encourages individuals to build and nurture professional networks, leveraging them for career growth, collaboration, and the exchange of valuable insights.

"Power of Reciprocity: Leveraging Favors Wisely" delves into the dynamics of give-and-take in professional relationships. This section emphasises the strategic use of reciprocity, encouraging individuals to offer help genuinely and leverage favors wisely for mutual benefit and strengthened professional bonds.

In essence, "Steering Relationships" is a guide to mastering the art and science of interpersonal connections. By understanding the principles of rapport-building, strategic networking, and the power of reciprocity, individuals can navigate the intricate landscape of professional relationships, fostering collaboration, trust, and mutual success.

D: Effective Questions to Ask the Leaders

- How do you recommend building strong relationships with colleagues and superiors in the workplace?
- What strategies can I use to establish rapport with clients or external stakeholders?
- Are there any specific cultural or communication nuances I should be aware of when building rapport with diverse team members?
- Can you share any personal experiences or anecdotes where building strong rapport had a significant impact on professional success?
- What are some effective ways to show genuine interest and support for colleagues' professional growth and well-being?
- How do you navigate and build rapport with individuals who have different communication styles or personalities?
- What are some key professional networking events or organisations in our industry that I should consider attending or joining?
- How can I effectively leverage online networking platforms like LinkedIn to expand my professional network?
- Are there any internal networking opportunities or initiatives within the company that I should be aware of?
- Can you provide guidance on how to approach and initiate conversations with industry experts or senior professionals during networking events?
- What strategies can I use to make a memorable impression and stand out during professional networking interactions?

- How can I maintain and nurture my professional network over time?
- In what situations is it appropriate to ask for a favor from a colleague or superior, and how can I do it respectfully?
- Can you provide examples of favors that are commonly exchanged in our workplace or industry?
- How can I ensure that I am not taking advantage of someone's goodwill when leveraging a favor?
- Are there any best practices or tips for effectively communicating my needs or expectations when asking for a favor?
- How can I reciprocate and show appreciation for the favors I receive from others?
- Can you share any experiences or insights on how leveraging favors has positively impacted your career or the careers of others?

Chapter VIII

Ethical Landscapes

Why this Chapter?

Ethics and integrity are like the solid ground on which a career story unfolds. When people make their career choices, keep their interactions honest, and handle tricky ethical situations with finesse, they're not just building a path to personal success. They're also adding value to their industries and the communities they're a part of.

Think about it as a ripple effect. When ethics are at the forefront of career decisions, it's like sending out positive waves that touch everyone around. And when integrity is at the core of interactions, it's like adding a layer of trust that strengthens relationships.

Dealing with ethical dilemmas isn't just about getting through them; it's about approaching them with a mindset that's open to growth and change. It's a bit like transforming your way of thinking from a fixed trait to an evolving outlook.

So, remember, ethics and integrity aren't just buzzwords; they're the building blocks of a career journey that's both fulfilling for you and impactful for others. It's like setting out on a path that not only takes you forward but also helps you leave a positive mark along the way.

A: Compass of Ethics in Career Decisions

When you're faced with career decisions, ethics become your compass. Graduates often run into situations where they have to choose between options that might not match their own values. That's when having a solid ethical foundation comes in handy. It's like having a trusted guide that helps you pick the path that aligns with your beliefs and where you want to go in the long run.

So, how does this work? Imagine you're at a crossroads in your career. You've got different paths to choose from, but some of them might not sit well with your inner values. That's when your ethical compass steps in. It helps you weigh the impact of your choices on yourself, the people you work with, and the world around you.

By making decisions that align with your principles, you're not just setting yourself up for career success; you're also making sure you're doing the right thing. It's like plotting a course that's not just about personal gain but about creating a positive impact on everyone involved. So, as you navigate the twists and turns of your career journey, let your ethics be the guiding light that ensures you're not just moving forward but moving in the right direction.

Example: Imagine a graduate who has just completed her master's degree in environmental science. She has received two job offers – one from a well-known energy company that has been criticised for its environmental practices, and the other from a smaller renewable energy startup dedicated to sustainability. The graduate faces a significant ethical dilemma: choosing financial stability and a renowned company or aligning with her personal values of environmental protection. In this scenario, ethics play a pivotal role in the graduate's decision-making process. She carefully evaluates the ethical implications of each choice, considering the long-term impact of her decision on her career trajectory and the environment. Ultimately, the graduate opts for the renewable energy startup, demonstrating how ethics guide career decisions by prompting individuals to align their choices with their values and principles.

B: Upholding Integrity: A Cornerstone of Professionalism

Maintaining integrity and professionalism is incredibly important every step of the way. Whether you're talking to your professors, colleagues, mentors, or folks in the industry, showing integrity is like laying the groundwork for trust and respect.

Integrity means being truthful, open, and keeping things consistent in how you act and communicate. When you hold onto these values, you're basically saying, "Hey, you can count on me." It's like building a reputation as someone dependable and trustworthy, both in your personal and professional life.

Being ethical in your behaviour doesn't just boost your image, though. It ripples out and actually makes a positive impact on the community you're a part of. So, remember, no matter where you are in your journey, whether it's the classroom or the office, holding onto your integrity and professionalism is like putting down strong roots that help you grow in the right direction.

Example: Consider the case of Alex; his team members suggest a shortcut that involves misrepresenting data in their presentation to make their proposal seem more appealing to investors. Despite the pressure to conform, Alex maintains his integrity. He discusses his concerns with his team, explaining that such an approach goes against his values of honesty and transparency. Although initially met with resistance, Alex's commitment to integrity earns the respect of his peers. In this situation, Alex's actions showcase how upholding integrity and professionalism in interactions can create a positive impact and establish him as a trustworthy and principled team member.

C: Ethical Dilemmas: Guiding Principles for Choices

In the world of careers, you'll often come across tricky ethical situations. These challenges can be puzzling and demand you to think deeply before making a choice. Graduates, especially, need to be ready to tackle moments when their values clash with outside pressures or conflicting interests. It's like walking a tightrope between what you believe in and the demands of the situation.

So, how do you handle these ethical dilemmas? It's like solving a puzzle. You weigh your options, think about the potential outcomes, and then make a decision that lines up with your inner compass—the values that guide you. This isn't just about showing your character's strength; it's about getting ready for roles where you'll be looked up to for leadership. You might find yourself making choices that don't just impact you but also the people around you, your workplace, and even society as a whole.

In a way, it's like honing your decision-making skills in an ethical gym. You're flexing your ethical muscles by choosing the path that's true to your beliefs. And as you exercise these skills early on, you're setting yourself up for roles where you'll need to make big decisions with a broader impact.

So, remember, facing ethical challenges head-on isn't just about getting through the day—it's about building a foundation of principles that will guide you through your career journey. And as you make choices that stand the test of your values, you're also shaping yourself into a leader who'll make a positive impact on the world.

Example: Imagine Sarah, a psychologist, conducting research on a sensitive topic involving participants who have experienced trauma. Sarah discovers that some participants have misrepresented their experiences in the interviews, potentially compromising the accuracy of her findings. Faced with an ethical dilemma, Sarah grapples with the choice of whether to proceed with the data, knowing it might lead to skewed conclusions, or to address the issue and risk offending the participants. Sarah decides to approach the situation with transparency and empathy. She contacts the participants, explaining the importance of accurate data and offering them the opportunity to revise their responses. Sarah's principled approach demonstrates her ability to navigate ethical challenges by prioritizing the integrity of her research over convenience, thus upholding the standards of her field.

Conclusion

"Compass of Ethics in Career Decisions" serves as a guide for individuals navigating their professional journeys. This section emphasizes the importance of ethical considerations in career decisions, urging individuals to align their choices with values and principles that contribute to personal and professional integrity.

"Upholding Integrity: A Cornerstone of Professionalism" explores the pivotal role of integrity in professional conduct. This section underscores that maintaining ethical standards is fundamental to building trust, credibility, and sustainable success in any career.

"Ethical Dilemmas: Guiding Principles for Choices" delves into the complexities of ethical decision-making. This section equips individuals with guiding principles to navigate ethical dilemmas, emphasizing the importance of considering consequences, values, and long-term impacts when faced with challenging choices.

In essence, "Ethical Landscapes" provides a moral compass for individuals navigating the professional terrain. By understanding the significance of ethics in career decisions, upholding integrity as a cornerstone of professionalism, and developing principles to guide ethical choices, individuals can foster a workplace culture grounded in ethical considerations, contributing to personal growth and the betterment of the professional community

D: Effective Questions to Ask the Leaders

- How does the company prioritize ethical considerations when making strategic decisions?
- Can you share an example of a situation where ethical principles influenced a significant career decision within the organization?
- What advice do you have for employees in navigating career choices that align with their personal values and the company's ethical standards?
- How does the company support employees in making difficult career decisions that involve ethical considerations?
- How does the company foster a culture of integrity and professionalism among employees?
- Can you provide examples of how employees have demonstrated exceptional integrity in their interactions with clients or colleagues?
- What resources or training opportunities are available for employees to enhance their understanding of ethical behavior and professionalism?
- How does the company approach addressing ethical dilemmas that employees may encounter in their roles?
- Can you share a case where an employee effectively navigated a challenging ethical dilemma while maintaining the company's values?
- What role do ethical guidelines and policies play in helping employees make principled choices when faced with conflicting interests?
- How does the company encourage employees to balance their personal ethical beliefs with the company's values?
- What steps can employees take to voice concerns when they believe an action may conflict with their personal ethics or the company's ethical standards?
- Can you provide examples of instances where employees successfully advocated for ethical adjustments in projects or decisions?

- How does leadership set an example in promoting ethical behavior throughout the organization?
- What strategies does the company employ to ensure that ethical considerations are integrated into the decision-making process at all levels?
- Can you share an instance where ethical considerations led to a more sustainable and positive outcome for the company?
- How does the company encourage ongoing learning and discussion around ethics and integrity among employees?
- Are there opportunities for employees to engage in workshops or seminars related to ethical leadership and decision-making?
- How can employees seek guidance when faced with ethical uncertainties or dilemmas that may arise in their roles?
- In your opinion, what are the key attributes that make an employee a strong advocate for ethics and integrity within the organization?

Chapter IX

Crafting your Identity

Why this Chapter?

Crafting a distinct identity holds immense significance within a professional setting, shaping not only how colleagues and clients perceive you but also establishing your presence beyond the tangible outcomes of your work or its societal impact.

Within this transformative chapter, we embark on a journey into the intricate process of building a dynamic and influential professional identity. Aimed particularly at early career professionals venturing into their occupational paths, this chapter underscores the pivotal role of consciously molding and projecting one's identity as a potent instrument for achieving success and fostering personal growth. The exploration unfolds across three key sections, delving into the realms of personal branding, navigating the digital landscape, and the fundamental virtue of authenticity in crafting a unified and resonant professional identity.

A: Personal Branding: Showcasing Skills and Passions

We often strive to excel in our work, and while that's important, the secret sauce behind that success is often our skills. Skills are like tools you can build and proudly display. Believe it or not, most of us have additional skills that can be super useful in other areas, but we tend to get so wrapped up in our own tasks that we forget to showcase these hidden talents to our colleagues.

That's where the magic happens. Imagine stepping up and taking on a challenging task from a different department, using your unique skills to help their team. It's like being the person everyone turns to for a specific kind of expertise. You know, like calling in the marketing whiz who's also great with numbers to help out the finance team, or bringing in the finance guru with a knack for creative ideas to spice up the marketing efforts. These instances are more common than you'd think in companies.

But here's the kicker: until you actually put those skills on display, it's hard to build your own personal brand within the organization. And that's where being versatile comes into play.

Now, let's talk about connections. We humans are social creatures, right? We tend to bond with people who share our interests and passions. Here's the twist—professional relationships don't always have to be solely about work goals. They can also feed into your personal passions, like cooking, reading, trekking, sports, dancing, music, writing, or even social work. Sharing these interests adds depth to your personality and shows that you're more than just a work machine.

These connections formed through shared passions can make your work life richer. They can turn mundane tasks into something exciting. And guess what? They can also be a lifeline when you need support from different departments. So, as you journey through your career, remember that your skills and your passions are your secret weapons. They not only make you a standout professional but also a more interesting and dynamic person in the eyes of your colleagues.

B: Digital Landscape: Social Media and Linkedin Networking

In today's digital age, our online presence matters a lot, especially on social media platforms. What we post, like, and follow can shape how others see us, including potential employers. It's important to use these platforms carefully because what we share might affect our professional image and relationships. Sometimes, even personal opinions can impact how a company views an employee, and vice versa. So, it's smart to be mindful of what you share online and to maintain a certain level of professionalism.

LinkedIn is a particularly powerful platform for building professional connections and can be incredibly useful for those just starting their careers. It can open doors to new opportunities and give your career a boost with the help of AI. For instance, LinkedIn's AI tools can suggest suitable job roles and make it easier to find and connect with potential employers. But remember, creating an impressive LinkedIn profile takes time and consistent effort towards your goals. For recent graduates, LinkedIn can be a great way to connect with successful alumni and colleagues to learn from their experiences.

Moreover, LinkedIn offers a feature called OpenToWork, which tells recruiters and your network that you're open to new job offers. It's a valuable tool, especially when you're starting your career. However, building a strong profile and network on LinkedIn requires dedication and patience. It's an investment that can pay off in the long run, helping you kickstart your career in the right direction.

C: Authenticity: Creating a Cohesive Personal Brand

Absolutely, staying true to yourself is vital, especially in a professional setting. It's natural to have insecurities and feel compelled to impress others, but trying to copy someone else's style or imitating their success can backfire. People can often see through such attempts, and it might actually lead to the opposite of what you intend – instead of admiration, it could result in a lack of authenticity.

Each of us has a unique combination of skills, qualities, and attributes that make us who we are. Embracing your individuality and focusing on what makes you unique is far more attractive and appealing than trying to be someone you're not. Authenticity is a powerful trait that radiates confidence and self-assuredness. When you're genuine and comfortable in your own skin, it's easier for others to connect with you and appreciate your contributions.

Rather than trying to fit into someone else's mould, invest your energy in exploring what genuinely resonates with you. Pursue interests and skills that align with your goals and values. This authenticity not only helps you build a sense of confidence but also makes you stand out in a meaningful way. Your individuality and the authentic contributions you bring to the table are what can set you apart on your career journey.

Conclusion

"Personal Branding" emphasises the significance of showcasing skills and passions to create a distinct professional identity. This section guides individuals in identifying their unique strengths, aligning them with their passions, and effectively communicating their value proposition to the professional world.

"Digital Landscape" explores the role of social media and LinkedIn in shaping personal and professional identities. This section underscores the importance of strategic online presence, networking, and leveraging digital platforms to enhance visibility, connect with industry peers, and showcase expertise.

"Authenticity" serves as the cornerstone for creating a cohesive personal brand. This section advocates for genuine self-representation, aligning personal values with professional pursuits. Embracing authenticity fosters trust, credibility, and a lasting impact on one's personal and professional identity.

In summary, "Crafting Your Identity" provides a roadmap for individuals looking to shape a strong and authentic professional identity. By mastering the art of personal branding, navigating the digital landscape with strategic networking, and prioritising authenticity, individuals can craft a compelling and cohesive personal brand that resonates with their values, skills, and aspirations.

D: Effective Questions to Ask the Leaders

- How does the company view the concept of personal branding in the context of employees' professional growth?
- Can you share examples of how employees have effectively integrated their skills and passions into their personal brand within the company?
- What role does personal branding play in employees' ability to take ownership of their roles and contribute uniquely to the organisation?
- How can employees effectively balance showcasing their skills with conveying their genuine passions and interests in their roles?
- How does the company encourage employees to utilise social media and online networking platforms to amplify their professional presence?
- Are there preferred platforms or guidelines for employees to engage with the digital landscape while aligning with the company's image?
- Can you provide instances of employees who have leveraged their digital networks to foster collaborations and learning opportunities?
- In what ways does the company support employees in navigating the dynamic and evolving nature of the digital landscape?

- How does the company define authenticity when it comes to personal branding and online presence?
- Can you share stories of employees who have successfully maintained authenticity while representing the company in the digital space?
- What strategies or advice can you offer to employees aiming to present a cohesive personal brand that aligns with their values and the company's goals?
- How does an authentic and consistent online personal brand contribute to building trust and credibility, both internally and externally?
- How does an employee's ability to craft an authentic digital identity impact their professional growth within the company?
- Are there examples of employees whose well-defined personal brand has led to unique opportunities or roles?
- How does the alignment between an employee's personal brand and the company's values contribute to their career advancement within the organisation?
- What role does an engaging digital identity play in employees' visibility and recognition within their respective industries?
- Are there recommended approaches for employees to maintain a consistent personal brand across diverse digital platforms?
- Are there any training resources or workshops available to help employees enhance their digital identity and personal branding skills?
- How does the company perceive the evolution of an employee's personal brand as they grow and take on different responsibilities?
- What are the potential benefits for the company when employees successfully manage to create a compelling, authentic digital identity?

Chapter X

Transitioning to New Horizons

Why this Chapter?

Transitioning is a phase of self-doubt and questions, which is a common journey we all go through. Whether it's switching jobs, industries, careers, or pursuing higher education, the path can be daunting due to one big hurdle: the "What if?" It's that little nagging voice that fuels our uncertainty.

It's interesting how this "What if?" has almost become a patron of the therapy industry. This industry has grown and improved over the years, and it's almost as if these two words have become a booming business. Have you ever noticed that?

Now, let's talk about the advice that's been passed around—find your passion, do what you're passionate about. It sounds great, doesn't it? But honestly, how many of us have a clear answer when asked about our passion? If you're anything like me, you might still be searching for that elusive "passion." And guess what? You're not alone.

I did a bit of digging, a small survey among the folks I'm close to. And guess what I found? Most people who are really being honest with themselves admit they don't have a concrete answer to what their passion is when it comes to work. Liking something or finding it interesting isn't the same as having a passionate lifelong commitment to it.

Let me give you an example. I enjoy watching MMA fights and diving into the world of food. When I talk about these topics, my energy and enthusiasm shine through. It's easy to assume that I'm passionately invested in them. But does that mean I want to spend my entire career in those fields? Not necessarily. I did spend some time working in the food industry, and while it was enjoyable, I realized it might not be the thing I want to do forever.

So, here's where my perspective shifted—from hunting for a passion to following curiosity. I realised that I, as a person, am evolving. My preferences are changing. What I'm curious about today might be different from tomorrow. Instead of stressing over finding that one passion to define my career, I started looking at what I'm curious about right now. It's become my compass, guiding me in my work decisions.

Life isn't a straight road; it's a winding path filled with twists and turns. And just as we change and grow, so do our interests and curiosities. So, the next time you're stuck in the "What if?" loop, maybe shift your focus from finding that one passion to chasing your current curiosities. It might just lead you to a fulfilling and dynamic journey you never imagined.

A: How to Approach: A Guide to Moving Forward

This part of the chapter in my view is one of the most important topics when you are planning to move or shift your career altogether. I will break down this into

1. Speed of learning
2. Saturation of learning
3. Experimental year
4. Importance of break

Speed of Learning:

Remember those school and college days when we all had to learn at the same speed? It often felt like a not-so-great experience, right? But guess what, the learning game changes once you step into the world of work. It becomes a whole new adventure, a journey that's different and, dare I say, pretty interesting.

See, the cool thing about learning on the job is that it's not a one-size-fits-all deal. It's like a buffet—you get to pick and choose what you want to learn and at the pace that suits you. Some folks might gobble up new skills like they're snacks, while others savor each learning moment like a fine meal. It's all about finding your own rhythm.

Here's the golden nugget: knowing how fast or slow you learn on the job is a game-changer. It's like having a superpower. Imagine this: you're working on a task, and you're thinking, "Whoa, this is taking forever!" Or maybe you're flying through things and feeling like a rock star. Identifying your learning pace is like having an insider's guide to understanding yourself in the work world.

And you know what's the coolest part? Once you figure out your learning speed, you can talk to your boss about it. It's like having a secret code for setting expectations. You can let your boss know what you need to thrive at work. It's like telling them, "Hey, I'm a quick learner and can handle a lot at once!" or saying, "I like taking my time to truly understand things." This kind of open conversation sets you up for success.

Start paying attention to your learning speed right from the beginning of your career journey. Think of it like training for a race—you're building your learning muscles. When you know how you roll, you're prepared to tackle challenges and opportunities head-on. So, my friend, as you navigate your career, remember that understanding your learning pace is like having a treasure map—it guides you toward a smoother, more tailored, and fulfilling journey.

Saturation of Learning:

Let's talk about curiosity—it's like an exciting adventure waiting to happen. Every job and industry is a treasure chest of knowledge about how businesses work and how people use products and services. But you know what's interesting? When we reach a point of saturation, where we've absorbed all we can on a subject. The timing of this saturation is different for everyone.

Here's a little comparison to help you understand. Think about money and investing. Everyone needs to figure out how to invest their money in some way. Some folks dive deep into the topic, learning about it based on their interest level. They explore different ways to invest, like using brokers, services, or getting advice from friends. Eventually, they gather enough information to make informed decisions, and then they're okay leaving the rest to someone else. This knowledge about investing reaches a point of "enough for me."

Similarly, there's a saturation level for learning on the job and about the industry you're in. It's based on your curiosity level. Just like with investing, there comes a time when you've learned a lot, and you start feeling like you've reached your limit. This limit might arrive at different times for different people. Some might hit it after 6 months, others after 2 years, or maybe even 5 years. It's all about your personal pace.

So, the key is to figure out when you've absorbed enough information, and you're feeling that sense of "okay, I've got this." Identifying your saturation point is like unlocking a door to your next step. It's like saying, "Alright, I've learned a lot here, and now it's time to start thinking about what's next." It's all about finding that balance between soaking up knowledge and knowing when it's time to spread your wings.

Remember, curiosity is a beautiful thing, and so is knowing when you're content with what you've learned. It's like moving from one chapter to the next in your own career storybook. So, keep your curiosity alive, learn as much as you can, and when you reach your saturation point, open your mind to what comes next. Your journey is full of surprises, and it's all about embracing the twists and turns along the way.

Experimental Year:

At the start of your career, there's usually one big goal: to make a splash and show the world what you've got. Some folks do it by highlighting their cool job title and fat paycheck, while others showcase their impressive degrees. If you've got enough money set aside to cover your expenses for about a year, here's a thought: why not give something new a try? Especially if you're feeling stuck in a job, even if it pays well.

Now, let's talk about timing. Giving yourself just 2 or 3 months for this kind of adventure isn't really enough. You know how time tends to fly by when you're having fun and taking breaks, right? We're kind of wired that way from our school days, where summer holidays of 2 or 3 months were all about having a blast. But when it comes to making meaningful changes in your career, a bit more time is needed.

Here's an idea: consider working for free or maybe on a project that's got some incentives tied to it. Use your skills, the ones you've already got in your toolkit. And instead of waiting for those 2 or 3 months to zip by, give yourself a span of about 6 to 12 months for this experiment.

Now, let's get into some strategy. If you're absolutely sure about the industry you want to dive into for the rest of your life, then maybe you can think about experimenting every 5 to 10 years, depending on your job. But here's the kicker: if you're not totally convinced about the industry, if you're still figuring things out, try shaking things up every 2 to 5 years. Give yourself that window of about 6 to 12 months to test new waters.

Remember, it's like trying on different hats to see which one fits you best. The career world is full of possibilities, and it's up to you to explore and discover. So, if you've got a little financial cushion, use it wisely. Give yourself time to experiment, to take those risks, and to find the path that really lights up your journey. Who knows, you might just stumble upon a career adventure that's even better than you imagined.

Importance of a Break:

Let's talk about taking a break, but hold on—it's not your typical vacation to a beach or a mountain trek. This is a different kind of journey—one where you wander through your thoughts, put yourself in unusual situations, and do things that need very little decision-making. It's about giving your brain a rest from the usual stimulation you get from books, people, and all the content around.

Imagine doing this for a few weeks or months. It's like stepping into a cocoon of change. You might come out of it as a completely different person. See, we often think that change comes from actively doing things, like forming new habits or taking up challenges. But as you grow older, you realise that not doing something can be just as powerful in steering your life in unexpected directions.

It's like working hard, but then taking breaks even harder. You're giving yourself the space to breathe, to let your mind wander without any pressure. It's a bit like a caterpillar that takes a break inside a cocoon before transforming into a butterfly. During that break, it's not flapping around—it's just resting and changing. And when it emerges, it's something completely new.

So, when you're considering taking a break, remember that it's not about packing your bags for a holiday. It's about giving your mind a vacation from the usual grind and letting it explore the uncharted. It's a break that can change the course of your life, all by not actively doing anything. It's like learning the art of working hard and then stepping back to allow the magic of change to unfold.

B: Self-Reflection: Paving Your Career Path

This is like touching on a specific point of your career aspect so far and how you can leverage it for the future.

Assess your skills and experiences: Take the time to identify and write out your past skills and experiences. This will help you understand your strengths and areas of expertise.

Identify your strengths: Reflect on your personal strengths and what sets you apart from others. Consider your unique skills, qualities, and attributes that can contribute to a job.

Identify your interests: Think about your curiosity and what truly interests you. Consider the subjects, activities, or industries that you find most engaging and fulfilling.

Consider your values: Reflect on your personal values and what is important to you in a job. Think about the work environment, company culture, and ethical considerations that align with your values.

Clarify your goals: Determine what you want to achieve in your career. Set clear goals and objectives that can guide your job search and help you stay focused.

Reflect on past experiences: Think about your past job experiences and what you enjoyed or disliked about them. Consider the tasks, responsibilities, and work environments that brought out the best in you.

Consider your work preferences: Reflect on your work preferences, such as your preferred work style, level of autonomy, and collaboration preferences. Consider whether you thrive in a structured or flexible work environment.

Evaluate your work-life balance: Consider your desired work-life balance and how it aligns with your personal priorities and responsibilities. Reflect on the amount of time and energy you are willing to dedicate to your job.

Identify potential career paths: Based on your self-reflection, identify a few potential career paths that align with your skills, interests.

C: Navigating Company Fit: What to Seek

Company history: Understanding a company's history can give you a glimpse into its stability, values, and culture. Find out as much as you can about a potential employer from press releases, websites, and social media accounts. Some important things to look for include how long the company has been in business and whether it is expanding or downsizing.

Opportunities for growth: Consider whether the job offers opportunities for professional development and advancement. Will you be able to learn new skills and take on new responsibilities?

Salary: Consider whether the salary is competitive for the position and industry. Keep in mind that other factors, such as benefits and work-life balance, can also impact your overall compensation.

Skills needed: Make sure you have the skills needed for the job, or that you are willing to learn them. Consider whether the job aligns with your strengths and interests.

Personality fit: Consider whether the job and company culture align with your personality and work style. For example, if you prefer working independently, a job that requires constant collaboration may not be the best fit for you.

Company values: Consider whether the company's values align with your own. This can include factors such as social responsibility, diversity and inclusion, and work-life balance.

Impact on society: Consider whether the job has a positive impact on society or aligns with your personal values. For example, if you are passionate about environmental issues, a job in a sustainable industry may be a good fit for you.

Location: Location is a major consideration when figuring out what to look for in a job. Consider whether the commute is manageable and whether you are willing to relocate if necessary.

Job title and responsibilities: Make sure the job title and responsibilities align with your career goals and interests.

Benefits: Consider whether the company offers benefits such as health insurance, retirement plans, and paid time off.

Work hours: Consider whether the job requires late nights or weekends, and whether the work hours align with your personal needs.

Work-life balance and flexibility: Consider whether the job offers work-life balance and flexibility, such as the ability to work from home or adjust your schedule as needed.

Leadership and management: Consider the company's management style and whether employees respect their leaders.

Tools and technology: Consider what technologies you will be working with and whether the company has the right tools to do the job effectively. Artificial Intelligence has arrived, how to use it and integrate into work for better efficiency.

Conclusion

"How to Approach: A Guide to Moving Forward" provides a comprehensive guide for individuals embarking on new career horizons. This section outlines strategic approaches, emphasizing the importance of planning, adaptability, and a proactive mindset when navigating transitions.

"Self-Reflection: Paving Your Career Path" delves into the significance of introspection when considering a career transition. This section encourages individuals to assess their values, skills, and aspirations, aligning them with potential opportunities to ensure a purposeful and fulfilling career path.

"Navigating Company Fit" offers insights into the considerations for finding the right organizational fit during a career transition. This section guides individuals on what to seek in a company, emphasizing cultural alignment, growth opportunities, and values that resonate with their professional aspirations.

In essence, "Transitioning to New Horizons" equips individuals with the tools and mindset needed to navigate career transitions successfully. By approaching change strategically, engaging in meaningful self-reflection, and seeking the right company fit, individuals can transition to new horizons with confidence and purpose.

D: Effective Questions to Ask "Yourself

- What are my primary motivations for seeking new opportunities or making a transition in my career?
- How do I envision my ideal professional trajectory in the next few years?
- What specific skills, experiences, or achievements have prepared me for this transition?
- What steps can I take to proactively prepare for the challenges and uncertainties that come with transitioning to new horizons?
- Am I open to learning new skills or expanding my expertise as I venture into this new phase of my career?

- How can I balance my enthusiasm for change with a realistic understanding of the potential obstacles?
- What are my core strengths and areas of expertise that I want to continue leveraging in my new endeavours?
- Have I taken the time to reflect on my professional values and aspirations to ensure they align with my transition goals?
- What are the key achievements from my current role that I can carry forward to showcase my capabilities?
- What kind of company culture, values, and work environment resonate with me and align with my professional goals?
- Have I identified specific companies or industries that are known for providing the kind of opportunities I'm seeking?
- How can I research and assess whether a potential company aligns with my values and goals before making a commitment?
- What level of risk am I comfortable taking on as I transition to new horizons, and how can I manage potential setbacks?
- What potential rewards, both personal and professional, do I anticipate as a result of this transition?
- Have I considered a backup plan in case the transition doesn't unfold as planned?
- Have I reached out to my existing network for advice, insights, or potential opportunities related to my transition?
- How can I expand my professional network to include individuals who have experience in the new field or industry I'm entering?
- What are my short-term and long-term goals for this transition, and how will I measure my progress?
- How can I stay motivated and focused on my goals, especially when facing challenges during the transition?
- What steps can I take to stay adaptable and open-minded as I explore these new horizons?

Thank You

Enormous thanks are due to Alvin Desai, a seasoned sailor of the Maritime industry. His ingenious suggestion for the book title (Think Through) not only charted the course but added an exhilarating depth to the narrative that sets sail through these pages. Alvin, a true aficionado of travel and food, can be found curating his adventures on Instagram at @rollingnpitching.

A special shout-out to the multitalented Nihal Berde, the architectural virtuoso and visionary illustrator who breathed life into the cover, turning it into a visual masterpiece. Nihal's creativity is more than a brushstroke—it's an echo of the stories within. Catch a glimpse of his imaginative world on Instagram: @nihal_illustrates.

To everyone who has contributed, shared feedback, and lent their unwavering support to this thrilling expedition, I extend my deepest gratitude. Your collective efforts have been the wind in the sails, propelling this book from dream to reality. As I joyfully share this creation with the world, it's impossible to ignore the crucial roles each of you played. Here's to the voyage ahead—may it be as extraordinary as the journey that brought us here!

For upcoming projects and bulk orders (for universities, organizations, career counsellors), please reach out on www.abhishekdeochake.in.

www.ingramcontent.com/pod-product-compliance
Lightning Source LLC
LaVergne TN
LVHW041040150826
845672LV00001B/405